Edward's Odyssey

Edward's Odyssey

AN AUTOBIOGRAPHY OF
Edward Gallahue

1970

DOUBLEDAY & COMPANY, INC.
GARDEN CITY, NEW YORK

TO
Dorothy, Gloria and Dudley

ACKNOWLEDGMENTS

Though the content, organization, and style of this book are my own, I sought and received excellent help in editing the material for publication. My principal editorial associates and critics were Seward Hiltner, of Princeton Theological Seminary and the Menninger Foundation, and C. Robert Jennings, well-known free-lance writer.

Seward Hiltner's editorial work was especially helpful in the sections dealing with philosophy, religion, and psychiatry. Bob Jennings showed great editorial skill by assisting me in reducing the manuscript to its present length without changing my style of writing. I am deeply grateful to these two men.

I also want to thank Elton Trueblood, author and professor at large at Earlham College, for several things. It was his encouragement that led me to write the book. Later on he read the manuscript and made many helpful suggestions.

When the manuscript was in process, it was read by Karl Menninger, M.D., chairman of the board of the Menninger Foundation; by Richard C. Raines, then Methodist Bishop of Indiana; by Robert L. Gildea, Public Relations Director, Indiana Area, United Methodist Church; and by President Alexander E. Jones of Butler University. I extend warm appreciation to them both for encouraging me to continue with the book and for their specific and helpful comments on it.

All the tedious but necessary work of typing and retyping the manuscript was carried out accurately and diligently by Mrs. Jean Avery and Mrs. Estelle Romine. I am very grateful to them.

I am indebted also to countless other persons who, although in a more indirect way, have had a hand in shaping aspects of this volume. There are my many long-time associates in business. There are literally scores of persons in the voluntary organizations with which I have worked—including hospitals, mental health societies, church groups, psychiatric organizations, colleges and universities, and many others. And there are other people I have met, like Wernher von Braun, who have made a profound impression upon me. There are also personal friends. To name them all would be impossible. But they have taught me more than they realize.

Finally, I want to express gratitude to Dorothy and Gloria, my wife and my daughter, for their patience, forbearance, and support during the long period of this book's gestation.

Edward F. Gallahue

I strongly suspect that the only people who do not have mixed feelings about writing a book are those who have never tried it. And since an autobiography cannot confine itself to unemotional facts, perhaps the conflict rate is even higher. I do know that, in spite of the intelligent and critical encouragement I have received from several author friends of mine, I have never lost either my interest on the one hand or my hesitations on the other.

What, after all, does an American businessman have to say that might possibly be worth reading? Even if he has been successful in his business activity from the point of view of producing a sound, dynamic, and profitable enterprise, with good morale and a reputation for ability in management, has he anything to say about such matters that others have not already said?

On the other hand, if he happens to have been blessed or afflicted with an inquiring mind, and has had many ups and downs in pursuing what Freud called the "riddles of the universe," is this kind of religious, ethical, and philosophical pilgrimage worth recording by someone fully aware that he is not technically proficient in any of these areas?

After I had determined at least to try to put something of this story on paper, it finally occurred to me that it might be precisely the combination of these interests—and neither of them alone—that might make my account of some general interest.

I hope and believe that there are some elements of the unusual and the creative in my business career. But I must admit,

at the outset, that it contains some elements of the Success stereo-
type. I did not have to start as far down the ladder as some men,
but the business itself did start at the bottom. As the record will
show, I am aware that not every judgment made was sound; but
the majority proved to be so, and what emerged comparatively
early in my adult life was a reasonable facsimile of business success.

Even though, in the world of business, I was able to concentrate
entirely on the planning and conferring, executing and deciding
what had to be done at any time, I found it impossible for
business to constitute my whole life. Whether I was reading
Nietzsche or Fosdick, I was always seeking something beyond how
to succeed in business with or without really trying. These religious and philosophical explorations were never steady or
routinized. They were deeper, more intense, and longer lasting
at some periods than at others, usually when I was facing some
existential crisis. But they were never absent even in my most
blasé moods or self-possessed moments. I see this part of my
life as a search that still goes on, although I have found some
stability in many of my convictions about the kind of world we
live in, and about the kind of God who made and continues to
make it.

Another area that has deserved and received serious attention
during this long process of mulling whether "to write or not to
write" has been my serious acquaintance and even suffering with
problems involving mental health. Although these emotional
problems were focused on close friends and near relatives especially my mother rather than me personally, I am not igno-
rant, even in myself, of what neurotic trends feel like, and of
the agony involved in even admitting the need for help, much
less that of attempting to get it. Yet I suppose I must disappoint
all those who would like a dramatic "mental health success
story," where there is first the problem, then the best professional
help is sought and applied, everything comes out all right, and
the world looks lovely ever after. While I believe profoundly in
the experts and their expertise, my story contains no simple,
concrete or resolved happy endings. Mental health problems may
be biochemical, hereditary, physiological, etc., in many of their

aspects; but they are also and always problems of relationships among human beings. Tangled human relations can be improved; they cannot be sandpapered to smoothness.

Since I have come to believe that we human beings are more truly strong when we can confess our weakness, more genuinely respectable when we can drop our pride, and more sensitive to the problems and ills of others when we can stop denying that we have some of our own, I finally decided that my relationship to emotional suffering and mental health was an argument in favor of writing rather than against it.

While my studies have been and are serious, I trust they are not overly solemn. Although many have been self-directed, I have often sought and received excellent guidance from experts in many areas. Hence I am only half "self-made." I have too much knowledge of and respect for all these fields to believe that my own explorations hold anything more than amateur status. So I may disappoint readers in search of a businessman to impress the Ph.D.s. I am not a professional. But I do believe that amateur exploration of the purpose and ultimate destiny of man is a vastly neglected pastime these days.

It may be that my own deep concern, bewilderment, anxiety— and even, at times, desperation—about the nature and reality of God, the peculiar complexities of the Bible, the ideological legerdemain of so much of modern theology and philosophy will strike some readers as unduly personal, idiosyncratic or atypical. Perhaps it is. But I am some kind of "preacher" in one respect, namely, I believe that too many areas of American culture and too many Americans have stopped any true "inquiring."

If I have, in this book, a message, I guess it is a story of conflicts, problems, some successes, some poignancies, some humor—but above all, I think, a story of inquiry and exploration. I have *not* arrived, but I trust devoutly that I am at work.

Edward's Odyssey

One

I was born on May 12, 1902, in Irvington, a suburb on the east side of Indianapolis, Indiana, that had only a tenuous connection with the city. Indeed, since Butler University was located there, it was really more like a small college town.

There was plenty of space in Irvington, and open country was but a few minutes' walk. As a boy I was able to fish, hunt, explore, idle in the woods, and participate in many kinds of sports and games. I cannot recall ever being bored as a child. There was no need for parents to invent ways of entertaining their children, for there were always things to do. All of us had chores, and when they were over we needed no one to tell us how to enjoy ourselves.

My mother, Pearle Teague, came from a Quaker family. Her father had been a prominent physician at Richmond, Indiana, and all the children had gone to Earlham College. She was a beautiful, slender, naïve, and idealistic girl when she met my father, Philip Gallahue. He was her antithesis except that he, too, was nineteen and handsome. He evidently swept her off her feet with his worldly knowledge, which really wasn't very worldly but only appeared to be. He was far from worldly in the ways of travel and of culture; but he had a smattering of knowledge of business, politics, entertainment, saloons, and girls with loose morals. And he had charm to spare.

My father's ancestry was sound. My paternal grandfather, Phoenix Gallahue, and his brother Warren came to Muncie, Indiana, in 1850 as orphans to live with relatives. Their parents had been swept away by a typhoid fever epidemic in their community in Virginia. My father was the only boy among many sisters, and he was taken into the family wholesale rug and carpet business. He was an excellent salesman, but he made many concessions in order to be popular. This was the sort of person my mother married, against her family's wishes and much to her ultimate regret.

My brother Dudley, four years older than I, was a bright, round-faced, blue-eyed boy with dark-brown curly hair. He was a bundle of energy with ambition to match. When, because of my father's periodic lost weekends, the family's finances were in a precarious position, Dudley tried to compensate by his industry and reliability. Because he had such a great variety of odd jobs after school, he practically supported himself.

I had great love and admiration for Dudley; and though I didn't realize it at the time, he was also the symbol of a father figure for me. My appearance and temperament were more like my mother's and her family; we were tall and slender and more English than Irish in appearance, the Teagues having come from England, the Gallahues from Ireland.

As a child I had two traumatic experiences. The first occurred when I was three and visited my father at a sanitarium for alcoholics. Even though Mother was with me, I found the setting terrifying. The home was a gruesome old Victorian place with all the character of a haunted house. The interior was dark and forbidding, and we were met in the reception room by a fearsome-looking doctor with big, dark-rimmed glasses and a beard. After solemnly briefing Mother, the doctor escorted us down a long corridor to Father's room. On the way one of the doors was open, and we could hear the commotion caused by a recent arrival whose attendants were trying to give him sedatives and get him to bed.

We found Father overjoyed to see us and very contrite. He apologized for getting drunk and blamed it on his customers, who had "insisted" that he have a drink with them. I was to hear this same story, with minor variations, many times.

My second traumatic experience happened when I was seven. It was a hot, dry summer day, and the dust lay thick on the National Road in front of our house. I had just started across the street to my home when a motorcycle seemed to appear out of nowhere.

I was thrown into the air and landed with a sickening thud in a cloud of dust. Father, who was on the porch and saw the accident, rushed out and picked me up in his arms. There followed a long, sad time for me and the family. With a fractured skull and serious internal injuries, I lived on the borderline for weeks, and it was during this time that I found out how much my father loved me. There was no drinking or any other foolishness by him during this period.

My condition was so serious that Mother's sister, Martha, who was a Christian Science practitioner, also was called into the case from her home in New York City. Her faith helped to fortify the whole family. After many months I recovered and returned to school, where I had missed only one term. I was able to make up the lost work and continue with my regular class.

After my recovery Father reverted to his old habits, and trying to cope with him became the focal point of my problems. Father was a man of many parts. Sometimes he was kind and generous, and the birthday and Christmas gifts were there as promised; but at other times there was bitter disappointment. He never admitted personal responsibility for his actions, but always claimed that his misfortunes were caused by others. He particularly blamed his father and uncle because they were forced to curb his desire to assume foolish credit risks in order to keep their business sound. The heavy drinking bouts continued, and he was arrested several times as a result of his behavior. When he sobered up, he would often return to the police station with gifts for some of the policemen in the form of 3 by 5 samples of the rugs that he sold, evidently hoping to soften them up for the next encounter.

Father's behavior produced a climate that was bound to create anxiety for the family. The reactions of Dudley and me to the situation were completely different and no doubt helped to set deep patterns in our personalities for life. Without realizing it, Dudley seemed to conclude that, since Father was unreliable, a lot of other people probably were too, and that therefore the safe thing was to be suspicious of everyone. This led to clever devices to outmaneuver and outguess people, whoever they were, hoping to "outfox" them. My own reaction was to pattern my life after Mother's, but I magnified and distorted her virtues so much that

I began to set ideals for myself which I could not possibly live up to later on. Father's behavior did bring the rest of the family closer together with a binding power of love and loyalty. This love at home, plus the existence of my many friends and interesting activities, counterbalanced, to a great degree, my disappointment with Father.

In spite of the turmoil created by Father's behavior, Mother was very courageous in her quiet, Quaker way, showing kindness to Dudley and me and trying to develop a religious, ethical atmosphere for us. She was truly heroic in facing her disillusionment and disappointment with Father. She started reading the Bible to us at an early age and instructed us in the Quaker doctrine of the Inner Light, which stresses that there is a little of God in each of us. But, since the Quakers did not have a church in Irvington, Dudley and I attended the Methodist Sunday school and joined the Boy Scout Troop there. After a while, however, we dropped out of Sunday school, because we could not accept the literal interpretation of the Bible that was taught at the time. Some of the Bible stories we found simply unbelievable.

Later Mother became more interested in Christian Science, and we attended the Sunday services and evening testimonials. Dudley and I did not fare any better here, for it seemed to us fantastic to ignore the physical aspects of illness. If we were sick or suffered physical injury, we wanted to see a doctor, and Mother acquiesced out of consideration for us.

Finally, in 1914, after twenty years of marriage, Mother gave up any hope of rehabilitating Father and secured a divorce. This eliminated the existing tension, but at the same time it created a vacuum. My uncle, Edwin Teague, helped the budget with an allowance of thirty-five dollars per month. This, plus our home, were the total resources of the family. Mother was thirty-nine; Dudley was sixteen; and I was twelve.

After Mother's divorce, it would seem that the family would have been drawn together in harmony, unity, and a sense of purpose. This did apply to Mother and Dudley, but not to me. I mistook my new freedom from worries over Father for freedom from responsibility. This attitude prevailed for years, which could be called the years of discontent. It was first evident in school, where I had done very well in the first six grades. In the seventh and eighth grades, I was offered an opportunity to take some extra subjects, such as Latin and algebra, but I refused to be bothered. My work in even the regular subjects slipped, and my teacher finally had a talk with Mother, saying that I was brilliant but lazy.

I was not lazy, however, as far as activity was concerned. Besides helping around the house, I had various jobs after school and during the summer months. Before I was out of grade school, I began to caddy at the new nine-hole Irvington Golf Course. It wasn't long before I acquired some old clubs and began playing a few holes of golf myself at odd times. I soon became so fascinated with the game that I gave up all other sports, which was both a blessing and a curse. It was a blessing in that golf was a healthy game, giving me a keen competitive spirit and bringing me closer to good friends and warm fellowship. It was a curse in that it distracted me from other things I should have been doing—I cut school many times to play, and I ducked jobs here and there to get to the golf course. I found a happy solution one summer when I got a job at the course, which gave me a good excuse for being there.

I entered high school with mixed feelings. At that time the two nearest high schools were six miles from home. I enrolled at Tech, which was about five miles by streetcar and another mile by foot. All my friends had the same transportation problem, but they did not seem to mind it as much as I did. Moreover, I had to get up early and take care of the furnace the first thing each morning. It was one of those old-fashioned soft-coal furnaces that would fill up with clinkers which had to be removed, and then the furnace had to be shaken down severely. This procedure always raised a cloud of coal soot that managed to get all over my clothes and into my hair before I could get cleaned up for breakfast and school.

This routine usually put me in a disagreeable mood, and if in addition the weather was bad, I was thoroughly frustrated by the time I got on the streetcar. If I happened to run into a friend who was in the mood, we would frequently cut school and go downtown to see a movie or shoot pool. I must have avoided school one-fifth of my four years there. I forget all the disciplinary measures which the school invoked, but they included staying late to study, as well as doing some physical work on a brick wall with a friend. How I acquired three and a half years of credit in my four years, I'll never know, but when the four years were up, I decided not to go back for another semester. During my last year, I had won the Tech golf championship as well as the city high school championship, and at the time this was far more important to me than my studies.

While I did not learn much in high school, I learned a lot of other things, good, bad, and indifferent, during these four years. I worked at endless jobs: I carried papers, mowed lawns and greens on the golf course, wheeled cement, worked as a house painter and a carpenter, served as yard clerk at night for the Pennsylvania Railroad, then as a surveyor's assistant; I clerked in a grocery store, sold shoes, and was a night watchman at a funeral home. One fringe benefit of the latter was that there were often extra flowers around, and occasionally I was permitted to take some for myself and a friend for our dates. Also, occasionally, a friend or two would drop in, and we would pass the time with a poker or crap game. I remember the time the owner, still a good friend of mine, stopped in to find a crap game in progress and wanted to know "just what the Hell is going on." I probably had some other jobs that I can't remember, but I know I was never fired from any of them.

I had a few tastes of pre-Prohibition liquor and visited some of the speakeasies after Prohibition came in. In addition, I had my share of dates during this period and learned something about girls. One might think my kind of life would have harmed me socially, but I don't think it did. My associates had a simple code—if you were a good sport about the ups and downs in life, had decent manners, and did not lie or cheat or get involved in unnecessary gossip, you were all right. Besides, most of the girls I knew had brothers, and from this experience they knew boys were permitted a wider latitude of behavior. By contrast, while I was very active on my nights out in this period, I also spent several quiet evenings a week with Mother, during which we read together or attended a neighborhood movie.

In the meantime, my brother Dudley had done well in school. He was a good student and pitched for a varsity baseball team. He had part-time jobs during the school term and a full-time job in summer. One of them involved selling coal: first he would get enough orders for a carload, then arrange to have it unloaded immediately upon arrival, since he did not have a coal yard or place of business. Due to his low overhead, he could sell the coal at a low price. He would start taking orders in the summer, and before going out, he always washed and scrubbed a few small pieces of coal thoroughly, then carried them around in the pocket of a white Palm Beach suit. Whether anybody really believed Dudley's coal was clean, I don't know. Maybe his customers were just amused. In any case, he sold a lot of coal. He was very careful with his money and turned all that he could spare over to Mother.

At this time Dudley had one great disappointment. He wanted to go to college at Butler, but Mother did not feel we could afford it, since he was then helping support the family. He dutifully accepted her decision and took a traveling salesman's job, selling shoes, which turned out to be really difficult. By the time my four years were up at Tech, Dudley had been out four years and was well established with an insurance company as auditor, having served an apprenticeship with a firm of actuaries and accountants which made audits and examined insurance companies.

During this period, Mother centered her whole life on Dudley and me. With the exception of a few neighborhood friends, she had no other interests except reading. Dudley and I did not realize it at the time, but she was really too young to discontinue any interest in men or deny the possibility of another marriage. I am sure Dudley and I didn't help any, as we were jealous to the point of citing the shortcomings in every man she dated.

After my high school days, Dudley got me a job as an underwriting clerk with the insurance company for which he worked. The year was 1920, and I earned fifty dollars a month! Even in those days I could have made more somewhere else, but the job afforded me an opportunity to learn the general insurance business. I continued in this work for two years, but advance was slow, and I became dissatisfied and began seeking a change.

At about this time, my uncle Edwin Teague of New York City
retired as treasurer of a large manufacturing firm and wrote that
he was going to spend the summer on a cattle ranch in Colorado.
Since his two sons, my first cousins, were to be with him, he
invited me to go along. It was a coincidence that Donald, the
eldest, was the same age as Dudley, and that Jack was only a
few months younger than I. Donald was already a successful
commercial artist, illustrating books and stories in magazines such
as the *Saturday Evening Post*, while Jack was attending the University of Pennsylvania and planning to become a professional
writer.

Though the principal occupation of the ranch was raising
cattle, the owners conducted a profitable truck-farming business
in summer. I had mixed feelings about going, fearing that I might
be an intruder and that my cousins might share this opinion.
Also, though I was very grateful for the monthly allowance Uncle
Ed had sent the family for years, and for my cousins' clothes which
had been forwarded to us in the past, I was a little sensitive. And
though I wanted to change my job, I did not want to give up
golf, as I had finally won the Irvington Golf Club Championship
at nineteen, which was my teen-age ambition.

Another problem of making the trip to Colorado was money.
I wouldn't need any money after I got there, as my cousin Jack
and I would divide our crop one-third each and one-third to the
ranch owner; but I would need an extra two or three hundred
dollars for transportation and ranch clothes. I knew I could borrow it from either Dudley or Uncle Ed, but I hesitated to do so.
While debating the matter, I decided to go to the Kentucky
Derby, which cost very little the way my friends and I went, and
to worry about the money I needed when I returned. Due to one
of those odd turns of luck, I bet a six-dollar combination on
Zev, a long shot that came in to pay approximately ninety dollars
on the six-dollar ticket. I also won some money on the other
races and returned from Louisville $125 ahead. Shortly after-
ward, I got into one of our periodic crap games and won the
astounding amount, for those days, of $150. Since I now had my
trip financed, I quit my job and went West.

Leaving for Colorado was a new experience for me. I had

never been away from home for any length of time, and my
parting with Mother and Dudley was a sentimental one. I knew
that Mother particularly would miss me and that I, in turn,
would miss both of them. However, the decision had been made,
and I was looking forward to the novelty of the trip and living on
a ranch.

The trip from Denver to Yampa, Colorado, was made on the
old Moffatt Railroad, before the present Moffatt Tunnel was
completed. It traversed extremely rugged country, rising over the
crests of mountains, passing through endless short tunnels, and
crawling along the very edge of cliffs overlooking steep gorges.
It was pulled by an old-fashioned steam engine, and since the
train only carried a few cars the smoke and cinders poured in
throughout the trip.

Yampa, located in northwestern Colorado, was a little frontier
town with unadorned frame buildings. It was set in a broad
valley with mountains rising on either side. When I arrived, I was
met by Uncle Ed, Jack, Donald, and Tom Alfred, the owner of
the ranch. I made a quick survey of this group, since I had not
seen my relatives for several years: Uncle Ed was still distinguished looking, even in his western clothes, although he looked
older and a little tired; Jack was about my size, six feet tall,
165 pounds; Donald, shorter and more full-bodied, resembled
his mother; Tom Alfred was a tall, weatherbeaten man with a
handlebar mustache and looked every bit the western rancher.

We were driven to the ranch about six miles up the valley,
over a narrow dirt road, in an old Mitchell touring car. Upon
our arrival, I met Mrs. Alfred and her daughter. Mrs. Alfred was a
small, wiry woman, and her daughter was tall like her father. The
house and the outbuildings were situated on the side of a rising
slope, and one could see a mile or two into the valley all the way
to the railroad tracks. There was a mountain stream on one
side of the house and a grove of aspen trees on the other.

After depositing some of my luggage, I was shown to my new
home—an army tent set in a grove of trees. It contained two
canvas army cots for Jack and me, a little chest of drawers with a
small mirror, and a washbasin. I will never forget those first few
days, getting acquainted with my cousins and other folks about

the place. Besides the Alfreds, there was a family of tenant helpers consisting of the parents, a son, a daughter, and Bill, a hired man who was to work for Jack and me. He looked like Ichabod Crane. Besides getting acquainted, I had to learn how to harness a horse, handle a plow, plant seed, and irrigate a field. In recent years it had been found that head lettuce could be grown very profitably during the summer months. There was apparently something about the composition of the soil, together with the warm days and cool nights, that made it grow to giant size with choice quality.

Jack, Bill, and I were soon at work planting seed on about ten acres of land that seemed like a thousand before we were through with the job. We had to cultivate carefully between the rows of lettuce, one of us leading the horse and the other following with the cultivator. The rows were narrow, and whenever I led the horse it always stepped on my feet. At other times we had to go over the ground on our hands and knees, weeding the entire area.

Most of my days began by getting up at five in the morning and washing my face and hands in cold water. I then had breakfast in time to be at work by six, and I put in about ten hours a day in the field. This schedule grew monotonous, but there was nothing to do but make the best of it. I don't know what motivated my cousin Jack to get into such a project, since he was doing well at the University of Pennsylvania, and Uncle Ed's wealth assured him financial security. Donald and Uncle Ed, on the other hand, had reasons for being there, because Donald was doing some painting, and Uncle Ed was taking a good rest after his retirement.

Even though I didn't like the work and missed my family and friends, there were some redeeming factors. I was never in better health; I had a wonderful appetite; and I followed regular hours and slept better than I had for a long time.

The ranch house was the center of activity in the evenings and the scene of conversation, both outlandish and serious, on many subjects. Quite naturally, the Alfreds' world was almost exclusively limited to their ranch and the things that affected it. Donald, of course, was interested in his art and in reading the stories he illustrated, and he sparked the conversation with lively comments about the various magazine stories and their authors. Jack had spent a large part of his life devouring books, and this too furnished a background for broad-range conversation. Uncle Ed was well informed in the business and financial world, and he served as a sort of elder statesman. My participation must have been less interesting, since my experience had been centered around my family, fellowship with my friends, and golf.

At about this time I awakened to the fact that I did not have any particular ambition in life, and I became increasingly interested in the ambitions of the others. It seemed that, except for Uncle Ed, their goals were centered on achieving success in their careers. Tom Alfred wanted a bigger and better ranch. Donald wanted to go to the top as an artist. Jack wanted to be a writer. And Uncle Ed wanted to travel and see the world. These little inquiries made me realize it was time for me to set some goals for myself.

Besides conversation in the evening, we had some other diversions—horseback riding into the surrounding country, rounding up cattle, and an occasional trip in the old touring car. As the summer wore on, we found enough boys on the other ranches to organize a baseball team, and played one game with a team from Oak Creek, a small mining town nearby. On two or three occasions we went to a dance at Yampa. We had some Colorado moonshine which made Indiana corn whisky taste mild and mellow by comparison. I don't remember much about the dances, except that we had to go six miles each way on horseback to get there and back and that the two favorite songs were "Carolina in the Morning" and "Yes, We Have No Bananas."

As fall approached, Jack and I looked forward to harvesting our crop. We began to build wooden crates in which to ship the lettuce. The railroad set up an icehouse and refrigerator cars at Yampa in the shipping season, and we had to be prepared to ship our lettuce when it was ready. We felt that we were going to have a very profitable summer. The crop was in excellent condition, and there seemed to be enough for ten carloads. This would mean about two thousand dollars net for each of us, and I knew I would be proud to be going home with so much money.

Soon the great day came, with everything in preparation to harvest our crop. It dawned bright and clear, and we went into the field where we lined up enough crates for a carload of lettuce. Meanwhile without our noticing it, an ominous cloud had moved over the mountains and was about to obscure the sun. Within minutes, the air started to cool, and we had the biggest hailstorm imaginable. Some of the stones were as big as golf balls. We ran for cover, and when it was over, our summer's labor was over too, for practically all of the crop was ruined. We did manage to ship one carload, which helped to defray my expenses. Now we had hundreds of crates on hand to be sold. Most of the crops on the other ranches had not been hit, and it was a matter of first finding buyers and then transportation to deliver the crates. Before these sales were completed, Jack had to return to college, and Uncle Ed and Donald went with him. This left me to finish the job. During the last week I was alone, and I had some long, long thoughts which I shall never forget. One morning I looked up at the sky and the mountains and vowed that I would go home and study for a career in business, that I would succeed no matter what it cost in time, work, or sacrifice, and that I would never stop "until I have all the money I need, by God." This decision was a turning point in my life. I was twenty years old.

On the way home on the train from Denver, I noticed an advertisement in a magazine about correspondence courses offered by La Salle Extension University. The particular ad featured a course in accounting and pictured an energetic young executive at a nice clean desk, enjoying success and prosperity. For the exact reason intended, this appealed to me and, sensing that a knowledge of accounting could be very useful to me, I decided to enroll as soon as I got home.

Mother and Dudley met me at the station, and it was a happy family reunion. They shared my disappointment with the crop failure, and then Dudley offered to get me a job with his firm. However, I told him of my decision to stay home and study in order to prepare myself for a career requiring both some specialized and basic knowledge. They were shocked at my decision because, as I was to learn, they were depending on me to help support the family. I told them that, while I did not wish to be selfish, I knew I could be much more successful in the long run if I could acquire some additional knowledge and skill. With that, I wrote immediately to La Salle Extension and embarked on a six-month period of self-study.

I told my friends what I was doing and said I would not be seeing much of them before spring. Because I had not studied seriously for years, I had no idea how difficult it would be for me to concentrate eight hours a day. I also had to master all the material myself, with no teachers except those at the other end of the mail route. Yet within a month I began to get into the groove with my studies, and the course became exciting as I acquired new knowledge. Occasionally, I would take Mother out in the evening or stay home and read some of the books on psychology and philosophy that Jack had discussed at the ranch: John Watson's *Behaviorism*, Nietzsche's *Will to Power*, *Thus Spake Zarathustra*, and the essays of Arthur Schopenhauer.

John Watson's deterministic psychology stressed the fact that man was largely the product of his conditioning through his environment. Nietzsche seemed to stress the need for man to shake off the shackles of superstition and stop placing restraints on the strong and courageous by coddling the weak and inferior. He felt that Christianity was the worst offender, that the Christian conception of God was outmoded. And he dramatized his thought on this subject by the statement "God Is Dead!" I was then introduced to Schopenhauer's pessimism—that happiness was not positive but the relief from pain or suffering. These works seemed to verify what I was beginning to believe—that religion was based on ignorance, fear, and superstition of the premodern world, that God was indeed dead, and that man was just now coming of age and realizing that he was on his own and in charge of the world, for better or worse.

I continued to pursue my business studies, and by spring I felt that I understood accounting sufficiently to look for a job. I had already decided to reenter the insurance business, as it seemed to appeal most. It was principally a business of ideas and legal contracts which I preferred to bricks and mortar, machinery and merchandise. I decided to specialize in automobile insurance, for the automobile industry appeared to have a great future, and automobile insurance would surely grow with it.

Fortunately, I secured a position as auditor of a small insurance organization, the Security Automobile Association. It was difficult to get the job because of my age, just twenty-one, but my previous experience in the insurance business helped, and the president evidently was impressed with my sincerity. To my delight, I found that my knowledge was adequate for the job, and I had no trouble with the accounting problems or with the preparation of the various insurance statements which were technical and complicated.

During this period, I had a social experience that was minor in itself but that resulted in such a delightful evening I will always treasure it. It had to do with an invitation I received from a friend who was attending Hanover College, which is located at Hanover, Indiana, on a bluff overlooking the Ohio River. He wanted me to be a guest of the Phi Delta Theta Fraternity which, for their annual party, had rented an old sidewheeler steamboat for a cruise on the river. The trip started about eight in the evening and ended around 1:00 A.M. It was a beautiful June night with a full moon; and this, together with good music and an attractive girl, produced one of the most enchanted evenings I have ever known. It had all the romantic nostalgia of Mark Twain's days on the river, and I was able to recapture for at least an evening this great era of Americana.

For the next year or so, things went well for me at the office and at home. But then came a shocking experience. In February of 1924, I was returning home from a business trip to Anderson, Indiana, by interurban, which was the chief means of transportation in Indiana at that time. It was a bright sunny day when I boarded the car; I went immediately to the smoker, but since all the seats there were taken, I found a seat in the rear. I settled down to a conversation with the passenger who shared my seat, and we had only been traveling about fifteen or twenty minutes when I caught a quick flash of another interurban approaching us on the single track. There was a terrific crash, and as the cars met head-on, they telescoped through each other's smokers. The explosion of flying debris, dust, smoke, and fire and the smell of burning flesh, punctuated by the screams of the injured, created an inferno of horror. Both interurbans carried a second car as a trailer, which added to the force of the impact, and since the cars were wooden they caught fire immediately. The seat I occupied was badly splintered, and my left leg was caught in the wreckage. I don't know how I extricated myself, but when I did, my trousers were torn badly, and one shoe and spat around my ankle were gone. My fellow passenger must have gotten out ahead of me, for I did not see him. It was impossible to help anyone trapped in the front end of the cars, where the fire was burning furiously. As I remember, there were more than twenty killed and dozens injured.

I don't know how long I was outside the wreck when I spotted Paul Shideler, a golfing friend and a photographer for the Indianapolis *News*. He took me over to his automobile where I remained, except for making a telephone call to my home from a nearby farmhouse. Outside of the terrific emotional shock, I found I was lucky indeed. My left leg was badly bruised, but I was well enough to return to work in a week or so.

I well remember the adjuster for the Union Traction Company who called on me at the office and offered me a settlement of five hundred dollars in bills of small denomination. Offering a cash settlement in this manner was a psychological trick used by adjusters on some people, since the small denomination made for a big wad of bills. I was not taken in by these tactics, however, and put off a decision on the settlement for a few days in order to check with Dudley and an attorney. I was advised to take the money, since the liability for the wreck would be so large it would probably bankrupt the company, which it later did. I, therefore, accepted the five hundred dollars and thanked God again that I was alive to take it. Had I found a seat in that smoker, I would have been killed with all the others there.

The horror of that experience was another emotional shock that caused me again and again to ponder the vicissitudes of life. It seemed to me pure accident that I did not suffer a horrible death, and yet the first thing that I did was to thank God. Upon rational reflection, my act of prayer seemed completely *ir*rational, for I could not believe that God had chosen the people in the front of the car to be human torches and those in the rear to be saved. Certainly the ones in the rear were not morally superior to those in front; it could easily have been the reverse. This dilemma between belief and unbelief set up a tension that was destined to haunt me time and again.

Toward the end of my first year as auditor, Dudley and I began to think of launching an insurance organization of our own. By this time, Dudley had had experience with a firm of insurance company examiners. He had served as an auditor of a company and his present position was that of claims manager. Our plan was to organize what is known as a reciprocal insurance association to write automobile insurance. Under this plan, the policyholders would appoint a managing company, known as the attorney-in-fact, which would receive 35 percent of all the premiums, out of which we would pay the agent's commission and other overhead and retain the balance as our profit. The remaining 65 percent would be reserved for the payment of losses and adjustment expense. If these organizations secured enough business and were managed properly, they could be very profitable for both the managing company and the policyholders.

To create a reciprocal company, it was necessary to deposit $25,000 with the Insurance Department as a guaranty fund for the protection of policyholders, to add to what was available from the premiums they paid. The management company also needed about $25,000 to cover initial expenses and overhead until the company started producing profits.

Dudley made a trip to New York to present this plan to Uncle Ed and his attorney. He did a great job of selling the idea, for Uncle Ed agreed to put up $15,000, and one of his former associates put up $10,000. With this commitment in hand, Dudley sold $15,000 in stock to prominent businessmen in Indianapolis, subscribed for $8,000 of stock himself, and I took $2,000. It is hard to describe our excitement at the thought of having our own company. After a few months' preparation, the American Automobile Indemnity Association was born in February, 1925. Dudley was twenty-six, and I was twenty-two.

Two

One of the most important elements of any profitable venture is timing. Shakespeare put it aptly into words, but I suspect that it has been a part of most successful careers in all avenues of life.

> There is a tide in the affairs of men
> Which taken at the flood leads on to fortune;
> Omitted, all the voyage of their life
> Is bound in shallows and in miseries.[1]

The secret, then, is doing the right thing at the right time. Some may be so endowed by nature, some may just stumble into the floodtide out of sheer luck. In any event, it is difficult to be successful if one plants seeds out of season or does the right thing at the wrong time. Dudley and I felt that Fortune had tapped us on the shoulder, and we got "her message."

Dudley was elected president of our new company, and I was elected secretary. We then rented a small space with two cubbyholes for offices and small workroom. Starting a business of your own is an exciting venture for anyone, and Dudley and I thought we had an exceptional opportunity in the automobile insurance business. Automobile insurance was in its embryo stage with everything in a state of flux; no one seemed quite sure what coverages to offer, what rates to charge, or what rules to follow. Even the great national companies seemed to be stumbling around like ponderous dinosaurs with their complicated rules, rates, and policies which were exceedingly difficult for the average agent to understand.

Dudley and I drew on our experience and imagination to

create a simple method of writing automobile insurance. Our greatest innovation was a short, simplified rule and rate chart instead of the cumbersome book of more than a hundred pages used by the national companies. We also simplified our policy forms to make them more easily understood. Finally, as a special inducement we offered a 20 percent rate discount from the national companies, such as some of the other small specialty companies had been doing successfully.

In a short time we had office help and the necessary supplies and were ready to sell promises which, after all, is what insurance policies are. Insurance is one of the many promises men live by.

Dudley was in charge of sales and the claims department, and I assumed the rest of the duties. In addition, I also assisted Dudley in sales. It was my job to recruit and train new agents, while Dudley was calling on all the established agents he knew. I had no starting point except my imagination. I began by approaching some of my friends, who agreed to start on a part-time basis after their daily working hours. One illustrious agent among this group was Dick Powell, who was then singing with the Charlie Davis orchestra in Indianapolis. He had recently moved into an apartment just two doors from me, and we became good friends for life. He was very popular and doing well with the band, though he had not yet decided to make a permanent career in the entertainment world.

At this time I introduced a novelty into the insurance business that worked exceptionally well. We prepared a pad of insurance certificates called binders, which we left with the automobile dealers, whereby we assumed the insurance for one week free of charge for any new car purchaser who was not already covered. This device gave either me or one of our agents an opportunity to see the prospect before he bought insurance elsewhere, since he was receiving coverage without charge for the first week.

This program worked out so well that our competitors objected, saying that it was illegal to give insurance free. We were charging this coverage to advertising, and to me it made no difference whether we gave free advertising in dollars, prizes, or a week's insurance. We gave up the practice, however, because we did not want to get involved in legal proceedings with our competitors.

It was quite an experience to call on prospects who had never heard of our company, and, when asked when it started, to tell them "last week" or "last month." I always softened the impact of this answer by adding that we were under the supervision of the Insurance Department and had the same reserve behind each policy as every other company. Moreover, I said, we reinsured all risks over a thousand dollars. It is surprising how few sales we lost because of the newness of the company. What we lacked in experience and size, we made up in enthusiasm and hard work.

We picked up momentum as we went along, and I was soon spending at least two days each week recruiting agents in small towns. I found it easier to secure agents there, because the field managers of the large companies were inclined to breeze through the small towns showing little interest in developing local agencies. Sometimes I could see why, for I would often call on farmers with our agents and end up in the barn, up to my ankles in horse manure, selling insurance.

We had difficulty with some of our established competitors. They ridiculed the idea of our starting a new company and predicted woeful consequences, saying the company would go bankrupt, leaving the policyholders unprotected while ruining our own futures. Fortunately Dudley and I had faith in ourselves and the courage of our convictions.

My experience during the rest of my life was to vindicate this faith, for most things which I have accomplished have been against the mainstream of others' opinions. I do not mean to imply that a person will automatically be successful by acting contrary to established patterns or practices, only that if a man has an idea that stands up under careful analysis, it ought to be tried. Although Albert Einstein and Charles Kettering were in vastly different fields, each made a point of saying that most men's minds are closed to novelty by the time they are eighteen. When, years later, I sat next to Mr. Kettering at a luncheon, he told me that whenever he held a staff meeting, he did not allow the presence of any slide rules or other paraphernalia that might limit open minds.

All forms of insurance are simple in principle. The system requires rates sufficient to cover losses plus overhead, leaving a margin of profit. Of course, actual practice of the business requires professional knowledge, and Dudley and I felt that we had acquired that necessary knowledge and skill. Having successfully held responsible positions with others, we now felt that we knew enough to operate our own business.

The business continued to grow, and at the end of the shakedown cruise of one year, we found that we had made a profit, were able to increase our staff, and no longer had to run a two-man insurance company. We continued to make an excellent record; and Uncle Ed and his former associate, Frank Errington, began to make periodic visits to Indiana, when they seemed pleased with our progress. However, Frank had become enamored with the stock market because his listed stocks were making a phenomenal rise in the bull market of the late twenties. He was a great fellow, but he used to needle Dudley and me by telling us how much his other stocks had gone up. Dudley and I found that we could borrow enough to buy him out and give him a good profit on his $10,000 investment, which was 20 percent of the total capital. The next time he mentioned the performance of his other stocks, Dudley advised him that we would be glad to pay a nice bonus if he wanted to sell out. This he did, and we were delighted that we now had 40 percent of the stock.

By 1928 we decided that we could broaden our horizon considerably if we changed to a stock insurance company. Under such a plan the stockholders participate 100 percent in all the profit or loss. We found that the majority of the public and agents preferred this kind of insurance, because a much larger capital was required for the protection of policyholders.

Therefore we began negotiations with an investment house to underwrite a $250,000 stock issue. Under this plan the management corporation of our present organization would exchange its stock for the common voting stock in the new company, and the additional common stock would be nonvoting but share equally in profits. By this arrangement the small group of original stock-holders were still able to control the company, and Dudley and I would own 40 percent of the voting stock. We made final arrangements with an underwriting house to consummate the agreement, and we secured the necessary approval from the Insurance Department to reinsure the outstanding business of the American Auto Indemnity Association and take over the assets and liabilities of the company.

When we received the payment for our new issue of capital stock in July, 1929, we invested all of it in United States Government bonds, because we did not feel that we could risk any of it in stocks. When the stock market crashed in October, it was clear that we had made a most fortunate decision. As the depression wore on, it seemed to me that mass hysterical optimism had created fantastic prices on the upside and that, when the spiral accelerated downward, it created an equal amount of hysterical pessimism. As the best of the Greek thinkers understood twenty-five hundred years ago, it is hard to get out of one excess without getting into another.

At the depth of the depression, a book was recommended to me with the bizarre title *Extraordinary Popular Delusions and the Madness of Crowds*. It was written by Charles Mackay, LL.D., and first published in 1841. Bernard M. Baruch, who praised it highly, declared that its perusal has saved him millions of dollars. And James Hilton, author of *Lost Horizon*, saw it as "a sort of case book of human folly throughout the ages, with special reference to what we would nowadays call the phenomena of mob psychology."

This classic book gave me a penetrating insight into what had happened in 1929 and the convulsions that followed. The knowledge seemed to put me in the eye of the hurricane, where I could make reasonably sound decisions without being unduly distracted by outside forces. I agreed with Mr. Baruch that two and two still made four in 1929, and that this also held true during the depression. In any event, Dudley and I proceeded to manage our affairs on this basis. The economy of the United States was malfunctioning violently. But we were clearly not the victims of a catastrophe that might have swept away our people or impaired

our resources. We, therefore, went right ahead with our long-
term planning, expanding our business into the states of Colorado,
Ohio, Illinois, Kentucky, and Michigan.

An unusual opportunity presented itself in connection with
our entering Colorado, which otherwise we should not have considered at this time. It happened that we had an agency with
the AAA Club of Indianapolis that sold insurance to their
members with our company. The manager told me that the
Rocky Mountain AAA Club, located at Denver, also was considering entering the automobile insurance business. I therefore
went to the National AAA Convention held in September, 1929,
at West Baden, Indiana, where I met Mr. Clarence Werthan,
the Colorado manager, and offered him an agency. I was successful in securing the contract, and it was a fortunate arrangement for both of us. We soon became close friends, and we have
transacted millions of dollars of profitable business together.
My trip to Colorado to start the agency was quite a thrill. Just
seven years before I had left Colorado with no money and no
job after the crop failure at the ranch. Now I was returning as a
partner in a successful insurance company.

We next entered Ohio, Illinois, and Kentucky and, in addition
to many other duties, I spent a large part of my time traveling
with our managers in the other states, appointing and developing
agents. At this time my work became especially strenuous, both
mentally and physically, because it was extremely difficult to
build an agency organization for a new company over a large
territory. To be in one or more different towns every day was
worse than traveling with a road show.

Also, since I was a bachelor, many of the agents and their
wives thought it would be nice to arrange dates for me with the
local girls, who would join us for dinner and perhaps some night-
club entertainment. The number and variety of girls I met in
this way was amazing—blondes, brunettes, and redheads of all
shapes, sizes, and degrees of beauty—and so were the various
levels of their education and morals. It was the rollicking, crazy
world of the "Roaring Twenties," a world of speakeasies, bootleg
whiskey, bathtub gin, stock market speculation; an age of excitement and reckless abandon, unforgettably portrayed by F. Scott

Fitzgerald. It was a very different world from the present one of discontent, anxiety, rebellion, and preoccupation with sex, where millions participate synthetically through novels, plays, slick magazines, and lurid paperbacks. My experience with girls certainly added zest to my traveling, but it did not make my job any easier, as it was sometimes difficult to block out the experience of the night before to get down to the day's business.

After we decided to enter Michigan, I was sitting in one of the Detroit clubs, interviewing Bill Niven, a prospective manager, when the stunning news hit that all of the Detroit banks had closed. At first the men in the room could not believe it; then they went into a state of shock. We knew that General Motors, Ford, and other large corporations had a vital interest in the banks, and we could not understand how it could happen. After the initial numbness passed, most of us reached for wallets and counted our cash. I returned to Indianapolis that night and told Bill Niven I would let him know shortly about opening agencies in Michigan. After I talked to Dudley, we decided that the United States was here to stay, and we went ahead with our plans. I called Bill Niven immediately and told him to rent an office, buy a company car, and come down for the necessary indoctrination. It was a fortunate decision, since we were to be practically the only company in Michigan appointing agents and promoting sales for months to come.

At this time, Dudley and I decided that it would be well to have a large amount of cash on hand in the event other banks closed. Shortly after we placed the cash in our safe-deposit box, all the banks closed. In fact, I was in Denver conducting a sales meeting in March, 1933, when President Roosevelt's announcement about the closings came over the radio. Thanks to our foresight, we were able to meet our payroll, pay our claims, and carry on a progressive business right through the bank holiday. Additionally, by managing our affairs well during the depression and the bank holiday, our standing in the insurance industry was greatly enhanced. Although we were still a small company, and I was only thirty-one, we had come through our baptism of fire unscathed.

As I traveled about the country, I was able to make valuable contacts with leading figures in the insurance and financial world. One of the most important was with Mr. Best, founder and head of the Alfred M. Best Company, New York City, the Dun & Bradstreet of the insurance business. I well remember the first time I visited him. He was cordial and considerate and gave me over an hour of his time. Moreover, he must have thought well of our efforts, for we received an A+ rating for management, the highest rating obtainable. For years to come, I made it a point to visit him in January or February of each year, and I was thus able to get an advance report on the results of the insurance industry the preceding year as well as his forecast for the new year. This information was extremely valuable to me, because his company was the nerve center of all the fire and casualty operations in the United States.

When I was in New York, I usually also called on Joe Rovensky, whom I had met through Uncle Ed and who was vice-president of the Chase National Bank, in charge of their foreign department. His observations about business and investments were always helpful. I also followed up contacts with our leading competitors in the Middle West, out of which grew a strong trade association of independent insurance companies that cooperated in many ways and helped all of us to compete on a profitable basis. One important project resulted in the exchange of information on rejected or canceled risks. Before, it had been costing all the companies vast amounts of money to insure undesirable risks that had been canceled by other member companies.

About this time, we changed our name from American Automobile Indemnity Company to American States Insurance Company, which was not only a better name to advertise, but a better name to have when we branched out into the general fire and casualty business. During this period, Dudley and I were able to acquire additional voting stock, and soon we had voting control of the company. I became sales manager, in addition to my other duties, while my brother devoted all of his time to managing the claims department and the investments. Thus the responsibilities were divided more evenly between us.

While the business was making real progress, other events were taking place that altered my life considerably. In 1928 Dudley had married Katie Nunlist, a very attractive brunette. Since our family had been extremely close, Mother was not happy about the marriage. I feel sure that her attitude had nothing to do with Katie, but with her fear that it would break up our intimate family relationship. Thus as the marriage approached, there was some tension between Katie and Mother and probably some unconscious opposition from me, for, at twenty-six, I was to be sole head of the household, with all its attendant responsibilities. After the marriage, Dudley asked me to go to South Bend for three months to develop our work in the northern part of the state. I knew this was not a wise business decision, as I had more important things to do at the Home Office, but it provided an opportunity for Dudley to get settled with his new wife without family complications. Though I did not like the idea, I went along with it in order to cooperate with him. I don't think Mother minded at all, since she went with me and knew that I would be with her exclusively most evenings.

After we returned home, Mother became extremely nervous and entered a state of anxiety that was unnatural for her. During this same period, she became interested in astrology. Introduced to it by a woman friend, Mother consulted an astrologer both at her home and ours. She was a small woman who looked like a gypsy, with jet-black hair and black eyes. She was a very persuasive talker, but her hygiene did not measure up to her speech. In her home she had one room set aside for all the paraphernalia of her practice. She drew charts about Mother and made long prognostications with elaborate claims about the depth of her insight. I attended some of the sessions and decided that astrology was built on superstition, wishful thinking, and flattery. Everyone seemed to be a potential genius of some kind.

At the time this interest of Mother's began, it seemed a harmless diversion from her inner anxiety; but she began to take the prognostications seriously, and I felt that I had no choice but to express myself frankly about the matter. I advised her that no reputable scientist or astronomer gave even passing attention to astrology, and that no college or university taught the subject. I pointed out that a person's characteristics are inherited at the time of conception and not at the date of birth. Further, I explained that there are more than a hundred million different sperms in a man, and that each sperm carries a different combination of genes. It was nonsense to think that the planets conducted twenty-four-hour surveillance and sorted out the precise genes for every person. I did not like to disillusion Mother, but I think I convinced her that astrology was not to be taken seriously.

Soon she became more interested in Christian Science, and in this I encouraged her because I thought it might provide her with a helpful message. I took her to a practitioner at least once a week, and between visits she read the suggested devotional material from *Science and Health*. Within a year she became virtually obsessed with Christian Science and frequently had me telephone a practitioner for "absent treatments"; the practitioner would pray for Mother and hold in his mind the right thoughts on her behalf. The climax of this period came when, on several occasions, Mother awakened me in the middle of the night to describe her distress to me and to have me in turn describe it by phone to a Christian Science practitioner. I resented being awakened at all hours, and I felt both embarrassed and bitter at having to wake a practitioner at two in the morning to describe Mother's symptoms as though I were reporting to God.

How could Mother, reared in such devout Quaker surroundings, become so involved in Christian Science? The obvious answer was that her inner needs had become desperate. It suddenly occurred to me that Mother was looking for meaning just as I was, but we were looking in different places, she in the stars and religion, I in psychology and philosophy.

Finally, when I thought we had exhausted the possibilities of Christian Science, we began consulting leading internists and surgeons. When one of the top surgeons recommended a hysterectomy, Dudley and I encouraged Mother to follow his advice. I took her to the hospital the night before the operation, and I remember how frightened she was. I shared her anxiety. As it turned out, surgery did not improve her condition, but only added the strain of the operation to her burdens.

Mother thought that it would help her situation if we moved into an apartment in the winter so that she would be less lonesome when I was out of town. We then moved into a new apartment not far from our home. We had been there only a month or so when she had a severe fall on the ice in the rear entranceway, bruising her left shoulder and left breast. Her skin was broken in the fall, and an infection set in that put her in the hospital. This was before the days of antibiotics, so she had to be treated by old-fashioned methods, consisting largely of drinking enormous amounts of water, of intravenous solutions of some kind, and of direct application of antiseptic powder to her wound. She had full-time, private-duty nurses for months, and each day she had to go through a miserable experience of draining the wound, which finally sloughed off about one half of her left breast. Sometimes the pain was so excruciating that I had to be there with her when it was done, and I am sure that on these occasions I suffered as much as she did.

I was at the hospital either during the day or evening whenever I was in town, and most evenings Mother would ask me to read the Bible to her. Her favorite passages were the Twenty-third Psalm, the Ninety-first Psalm, Romans 8:37, 39, and Matthew 10:21, 30, and 31. Since our prayers never seemed to be answered, I felt that if there were a God, He was mocking us, and that when I read the Bible and prayed, I was the victim of a delusion.

One night as I was approaching my home after visiting Mother in the hospital, a couple of fire trucks rushed past, and I soon found that my own house was burning. The firemen had already broken in the front door and were pouring on streams of water both inside and out. It was still possible to go up the front stairs to my bedroom, where with the help of members of the Irvington Fire Department, whom I knew, I gathered up some personal belongings. The fire was soon put out, but it had gutted the center of the house, which was to take three months to rebuild. I moved into the Columbia Club and I felt a new awareness of Shakespeare's insight:

> When sorrows come, they come not single spies
> But in battalions![2]

I had a very difficult time adjusting the loss because, of course, I could not tell Mother about it. The only by-product of the fire was that I had Mother's room redecorated with new furniture, so that when she returned home it was much more attractive than before.

In spite of Mother's terrible suffering, she still had a spark of humor. The nurse that came home with us was extremely tall and thin, but she had a very pretty face, and I think that Mother was concerned that I might spend too much time with her when she was away from Mother's room. When a neighbor came by one day and remarked that the nurse looked like an American Beauty rose, Mother sniffed that she must indeed be an American Beauty rose since she had such a long stem.

Besides Mother's illness, I also acquired some perplexing problems with Father, who had remarried a few years before and moved to Chicago. His new wife was an attractive and cultured woman of Quaker background who had started a successful business career after her husband's death. She had known Father in his youth and had long been fond of him.

Evidently Father's business had not gone well in Chicago, for he returned to Indianapolis in 1931 and rented an apartment. He began dropping in at the office every week or so to see Dudley and me. He was very cordial and acted almost as if he had never either been away or divorced. I asked Dudley what manner of man this was. He deserts his family with no provision for their welfare or support; he goes to Chicago and marries another woman, dissipates most of her savings, returns home fifteen years later, acts as if nothing had happened, and is full of ideas and great expectations. I don't know why I wasn't angry with him, but there was always something about Father that was captivating and appealing. Besides, Dudley and I were doing well financially, and I must have felt sorry for him.

He had been back only a short time when he asked us for some advice on a friend's business problem. A Mrs. Allison had gotten in touch with him. She was the widow of Jim Allison, who started Allison Engineering and was one of Carl Fisher's partners in building the Indianapolis Speedway. Father also had been a friend of his and of Carl Fisher's. Mrs. Allison had known Father at the time he met my mother and had also been fond of him. Dudley and I called on Mrs.

Allison with Father, and we found that, even though she was wealthy, she had some complex business problems. Dudley and I advised her to get in touch with a leading accounting firm, since her business problems were out of our line, and I knew Father would only be confused by them. He probably realized this too, which is why he got in touch with us.

Later, without our knowledge, she turned a large warehouse over to Father. It was half-empty when he took it over, but within months he had it filled to capacity. On the surface things looked great, but he had offered to rent the space far too cheaply, and with the added overhead, Mrs. Allison was losing even more money than before. The same situation had occurred when our father was in business with his father: he did an immense business at a loss. Mrs. Allison finally got the matter straightened out with a change in management, but she did not blame my father for his mistakes. In fact she still had a mounted color photograph of him that was taken when he was about eighteen. She very kindly made copies of it for Dudley and me and also presented us with two lovely pen and pencil sets. After leaving her apartment we asked each other what in the name of God made Father so attractive to lovely women, such as my mother, my stepmother, and Mrs. Allison. Whatever his secret, we never found out for sure, but we did realize that, except when he was drinking, he was like a lovable adolescent, with no real sense of responsibility. He unintentionally hurt people by his thoughtless selfishness.

Meanwhile, Mother's nervous anxiety continued, but none of the doctors had a solution or even constructive advice. She was now nearly sixty years old, and it seemed to me that she had gone through a personality change. My love for her was now mingled with guilt feelings whenever I did not do everything possible for her. Because of her condition and my many trips, we decided that we should move into an apartment hotel downtown during the winter months, where she would have easy access to the clubs, stores, and movies. We did this for several years, and though it did not solve her problems, the atmosphere made her less lonesome when I was out of town.

Besides my added responsibilities for Mother and business,

I was caught up by a merry-go-round of change; even Irvington, for which I had a deep attachment, had changed. Butler University had moved to spacious grounds on the north side of Indianapolis. While this was a great step forward, offering a beautiful location, it left a vacuum in Irvington. The college buildings stood stark and empty, the athletic field, where I had watched football games since childhood, had grown full of weeds. During the days when Pat Page was coach, Butler played opening games with Notre Dame when Knute Rockne had the famous Four Horsemen in his backfield. The highlight of this era for Butler was the day it beat Illinois University even with Red Grange on their team. My friend Bob Blessing played end for Butler and caught the pass that won the game.

With faculty and students gone from Irvington, much of the civic leadership and color were gone too. The sorority and fraternity houses which had housed so much life and laughter now sat forlornly on quiet streets. Though I did not attend Butler, most of my friends did, and I had gone there in spirit; for years most of my social life was connected with it.

Irvington had, and still has, a tremendous community spirit and loyalty, but with Butler's departure it changed for me. This plus the fact that Dudley lived on the north side caused Mother and me to consider moving too. Hence in 1935, when I was thirty-three, Mother and I moved to be nearer Dudley. I considered the move with mixed feelings. Dudley could certainly be of more help to the family if we were in his neighborhood, yet my roots were so deep in Irvington that I hated to leave. The founding fathers of 1870 had laid out the community with care and good judgment. There were beautiful winding streets with lovely shade trees, and the residents had exercised great civic pride in maintaining their property well and looking after the community. Butler University, which moved there in 1875, created a cultural force that nurtured numerous civic clubs: literary, dramatic, music, political, etc. It seemed that there was a club for everything.

The number of distinguished citizens that emerged from that little community of about one square mile is amazing. At one time in the twenties, the governor of Indiana and a United States senator came from the same block in which I lived; Dick Powell, who later became a movie actor, director, and producer, lived across the street. Our future governor taught me to ride a horse before I went to Colorado. Irvington wasn't one of those places so popular with modern novelists where all sorts of sordid things go on behind the scenes.

The town of course had its tragedies and disreputable characters, but scandals and tragedies had a way of coming to the surface as general knowledge. There was the Butler student, the lovely daughter of one of the professors, who became pregnant by another professor, the father of several children. The girl committed suicide.

There was the eighteen-year-old brother of a friend of mine who, disillusioned in love, tried to kill himself, but managed only to blind himself for life, and then heroically fought back by learning Braille to gain a job. He and his mother used to call on us after his self-inflicted injury, and it was heartrending to see him use every resource to hold up his end of a conversation by his knowledge of current events and the books he was reading.

Another sorrowful event involved a friend who refused to go into the family business and became a motorcycle policeman. He was shot to death one night in front of his home, and his murder was never solved.

Then there was one of the most disreputable characters that ever lived, who decided to make his home in Irvington after buying one of the few mansions there. This was D. C. Stevenson, the Indiana head of the Ku Klux Klan, with the bizarre title of "Grand Dragon." This character was sentenced to life imprisonment after luring a lady acquaintance, who lived in his neighborhood, to Hammond, Indiana. En route there on the train, he ravished and criminally assaulted her—even tooth marks were found on her body; she died a few weeks later.

Thus Irvington was not all sweetness and light; it was no Shangri-la. It also had its share of thunder and lightning, of war casualties, accidents, disease, pain, suffering, and death; but still Irvington was somehow different—it had something built into the character of its people to sustain them, a sense of purpose, service, pride, and responsibility.

Mother and I reluctantly left Irvington after finding an excellent corner lot across from the new Butler campus, not far from Dudley. By this time I was in sound financial shape and secured a leading architect and builder to design an attractive French Provincial house. During the building and the planning of furnishings, Mother seemed to take a new interest in life.

The home and furnishings turned out beautifully, but at this point I made one of the great mistakes of my life and one that I have always regretted. I thought it would be appropriate to dedicate our new home with a housewarming, and I invited a number of my friends to a party. To make it a gay occasion, I arranged for Louis Lowe and his Indianapolis Athletic Club orchestra to play in our rather large recreation room. Everybody had a good time, except my mother. Though she looked wonderful, and I was proud of her, I found afterward that the party had caused her to be overly nervous and excited. I also think she felt that I had grown away from her as my world had gotten larger. I loved Mother dearly, and I should have invited her friends to a quiet dinner party, instead of turning the place into a night club on the very first night.

Three

At this point in my life I was leading four lives, not blended or coordinated, but each radically different—my life with Mother, my life of search for meaning, my business life, and my social life.

I added a new dimension to my social life in 1935, when I became interested in boats. During my trips around the state, I visited Lake Wawasee a few times, which always seemed to be an ideal vacation spot. On one of my trips, I acquired a Chris-Craft speedboat. That summer I could use it only occasionally, but it gave me a new interest; and at the lake I could relax with a sense of freedom from responsibilities not possible either at home or at the office. While there I stayed at the Spink Hotel, the only one of its kind on any of the Indiana lakes. Mr. Spink had built several buildings in Indianapolis, including the Spink Arms, where Mother and I stayed in the winter. After his death, the lake hotel went to his sisters, and one of them, Mrs. Cuniff, managed it. The hotel had been built in 1929 on a deluxe basis; it fronted on the lake and had an eighteen-hole golf course.

Other factors that contributed to the attraction of the hotel were a dance orchestra and a gambling casino. At that time, the whole layout appealed to me very much. I could drive from Indianapolis to the lake in three hours, and I greatly enjoyed the drive, as I had just purchased a Cadillac convertible. I could enjoy boating, fishing, swimming, and golf by day, and by night entertainment at the hotel or the Waco Dance Pavilion, which often attracted name bands. Every facility was convenient, and I could go anywhere on the lake by boat. With such a setting, the only other necessity was an attractive girl, and there was always an abundance of them staying there with their families or their friends. In addition, I knew the hotel hostess, Mrs. Carlos Recker, who always introduced me to any attractive girls who happened to be around. "My God!" I thought. "I have discovered a new Garden of Eden."

My social life was getting more and more interesting and complicated. I had recently been invited to join the Bachelors' Club, a group limited to ten members, a new one being elected whenever a member succumbed to marriage. The Club had no purpose except to encourage fun and social activities, and all the members were well suited to these aims. All of them were well educated, several with Ivy League backgrounds, and most were financially well fixed. While I enjoyed the various activities as much as any of them, they came at a high price physically and mentally because of my responsibilities at home and in business. Though all of my friends were employed, they were not carrying as heavy responsibilities as I was at the time. In any event, I enjoyed the fellowship and the many colorful activities. Among them were parties at the 500 Mile Race and the Kentucky Derby, plus the annual Bachelors' Club Ball for four or five hundred people.

Another Bachelors' party had to do with a ball we were asked to give in connection with the première of the movie version of Bernard Shaw's *Pygmalion* at Loew's Theater in Indianapolis. The manager asked us to act as judges in a contest to select a Pygmalion of the evening and to sponsor a Cinderella Ball. When we agreed, we didn't realize what we were getting into, because the producer and the promotion people loosed an avalanche of publicity, and the Bachelors were soon interviewing scores of girls. At least the interviews were decorous, as representatives of the press were always present when they were being conducted.

Although I am sure that my friends met a lot of new girls through this activity I did not take much part since I was extremely busy at the time. However, my involvement came after a girl was selected to be Belle of the Cinderella Ball. We had to furnish her complete outfit, and this meant that everything had to be charged to someone until the money came in from ticket sales. One of my friends thought it a cute idea to charge the clothes to me; and, unfortunately, Mother happened to open my bill that month and noticed the charges for all the apparel on my account, including those for personal undergarments. I finally clarified the situation for Mother, but not without difficulty. The ball turned out to be quite a success, celebrated with Klieg lights and all the fanfare of a Hollywood première, with about five hundred special guests attending the theater and the party afterward.

My visits to New York meant even more social activity. During these trips I usually managed to visit the best night clubs with an attractive girl. It seemed to me that I was getting the best of everything out of this city with very little effort. I think the philosophy I adopted added greatly to my zest and enjoyment—I temporarily suspended concern about the cost of anything. On the basis of pure value, everything was overpriced in New York, and if I expected full value received, I should have stayed home. Therefore, since my visits were of short duration, I felt that a few hundred dollars did not have any real effect on my financial condition, but that it did make a great difference to my enjoyment during my stay. I heartily recommend this philosophy without reservation. If you have the means, go to the best restaurants, night clubs, and shows, and don't spoil the fun trying to get value received. I might add that women also enjoy this attitude, unless it is a wife watching the family budget. Occasionally I would be joined in New York by a bachelor friend who had business there, and we would rent a suite at the Waldorf for entertaining.

Once in a while, I also engaged in another activity that provided some novelty, though it was perhaps too bizarre on one occasion. Occasionally after a party on Saturday night, a group of us would catch a TWA plane and fly down to St. Louis for an early breakfast. On one occasion, however, when I had been drinking too much, a friend and I decided to fly to Los Angeles and I woke up just as we were landing in Albuquerque, New Mexico. That was the last time I ever made an impromptu plane trip when I had been drinking.

Probably the parties I enjoyed most were those for which some close friends and I rented a special club and observation car to go to the Indiana-Purdue football games when they were played at Bloomington. The Illinois Central provided the service of a special car at the end of the train, and we always had a little three-piece band to entertain us en route. Some musicians occasionally made up clever limericks appropriate to each person. We also had a bartender and some waiters who, together with our group and dates, made it a gala affair. In addition we had insurance against the weather, since we could always have a good time in the car even if the weather was too bad for watching football.

On several occasions I invited some of the Bachelors' Club members to the lake. Once we were discussing the future Lambs Club show with some girls from Fort Wayne, and we felt they could add a lot to the show, since they were not only attractive but experienced in entertaining at their private clubs. One of the girls said she doubted if they could add anything to the show, but she did know a girl who was very talented as both singer and dancer. I asked if she could bring her over to the lake, where I could meet her and arrange for an audition with Jack Tilson, head of the hotel orchestra. My friend proved to be a good judge of talent, for the girl was Marvel Maxwell, who went on to movies as Marilyn Maxwell. She came to Indianapolis with several other Fort Wayne girls, together with the head of the dancing school there, who was formerly from Indianapolis. Dudley was chairman of this particular Lambs Club show, and though he was skeptical of using outside talent he had never seen, I reassured him and told him that it would be good for the show to have some new talent. As things turned out, it was one of the best shows the Lambs ever produced.

Since Dudley was chairman, I saved one of the programs, which were prepared by one of my friends in the advertising business; they satirized some of the leading Lambs Club members and their businesses. The following applied to our company, and the Bachelors' Club:

DRIVE CAREFULLY . . .

You'd Better, We

Seldom Pay Off

Try and get one of our very special convertible and collapsible live or die, survive or perish, non-assessible, non-convertible, non-collectable, non-participating Golden Rule Policies.

"Do others as you would not be done."

Dud Galla—who

Ed. Galla—which

AMERICAN SNAKES

INSURANCE COMPANY

"We Cheat You Right"

BACHELORS' CLUB

An Intimate Message

for	Are you steadily employed? Do you make at least 50 bucks a week? Are you, by any
GIRLS	chance, looking for a husband with charm,
of legal	culture and all that stuff?
age pre-	If so, please address Box 7-11 Bachelors' Club.
ferred.	P.S. Be sure about that 50!

ACT IX

"DANCE A LA SWAMP LAND"   with Marvel Maxwell

Marvel Maxwell was such a hit that she was invited to sing with the Columbia Club orchestra. She came to Indianapolis and stayed with her aunt. When Buddy Rogers came to town, she joined his band and went on to great success from there.

Occasionally, when I was at the lake and came in late, I would observe the night watchman going around checking the slot machines for coins left in the till. Not finding any, he would play the machine himself, and I expect he must have left most of his money there, since they are always set to favor the house. It has always been a mystery to me why these machines get so much attention, particularly from women.

Other amusing gamblers were the ones who had "a system." I remember a mathematics professor from a northern Indiana college who it appeared was in the casino every night; at least he was always there when I went in. He would bring along a little notebook and record every number that came up on the roulette wheel, but when he himself played he usually lost. All the house had to do to upset his system, had it been a valid one, was to spin the wheel after closing.

I used to visit some of the professional gamblers at the hotel during the day and occasionally take them out in the boat. They were rather fascinating, colorful characters, far more interesting as a matter of fact than some "substantial" citizens. They made no apologies for their profession because they felt it was basic to human nature to want to take a chance. There is a little larceny and greed in all of us and a desire to get something for nothing; they simply were clever at exploiting this weakness in human nature. We never discussed the morals of gambling, though we did agree that the compulsive gambler is dominated by an irresistible force and is never excited unless he is flirting with financial disaster. This, we felt, applied regardless of a person's wealth; the bets simply had to be big in proportion to a person's means. I had a friend in this category, and once at the Kentucky Derby he placed an unusually large bet on Count Fleet, an outstanding favorite. The horse won by eight or ten lengths, but my friend was so nervous after winning that he ran down to the men's room to vomit!

Another friend, formerly in the Army Air Force, operated an airplane sight-seeing and taxi service at the lake hotel, and once in a while I would be sitting around with a girl with nothing much to do and make a silly remark like, "Let's get Bob to fly us through that cloud bank in the sky!" And quite often we would take off on a little adventure like this.

At other times, I would take my favorite waiter, Burnsides, on the boat at night to mix drinks while I visited around the lake. He had been a waiter on the Super-Chief and liked to talk about the celebrities he had served. He was quite good-natured, and yet phony in some ways, including his work habits. Before he could be seen by his diners, he was indolent and lazy; but as soon as he came into view, he would break into a dogtrot and appear to be out of breath when he arrived at the table.

One night, when I, my date, and another couple had been drinking too many of Burnsides's concoctions, we arrived at the Waco Dance Pavilion just before the dance was over. In order not to miss the music, I told the band leader to let the crowd get away, and that I would rent the orchestra for another hour or so. This I did, but we wound up with one couple dancing and my sitting at the table talking to my date. Liquor affects people differently. In my case, the music always seemed to get better; the girls got prettier; I thought I was a great lover; and I felt wealthier and wiser. I talked about everything from romance to the founding fathers, from philosophy of life to the accident of birth. I don't know why the girls listened to me, unless it was that they were affected the same way.

In my business life, I became deeply interested in one of the problems facing the agency type automobile insurance companies. They were losing business to insurance companies that were writing finance business. Most of the major automobile manufacturers had an arrangement whereby they would finance and insure the car at the time it was sold by their dealers. Thus I conceived the idea of starting our own finance company for insurance agents. I discussed this matter with Dudley, and he was enthusiastic about it, since it would not only help our insurance business, but would add a profitable *new* business.

To make a profit in the finance business, it is not only necessary to loan the stockholders' money, but to borrow several times the capital at a low rate of interest and loan it at a higher rate. One way to accomplish this is to borrow money from banks by putting up the loans as collateral. Therefore, before we could start a finance company, we had to arrange for credit lines of at least two million dollars. When I first talked to the bankers, they looked at me with fishy eyes and wondered how I was ever going to teach hundreds of agents in hundreds of different towns in six states to make loans without on-the-spot supervision. I had anticipated this question and had planned my answer carefully. Reliable agents know almost as much about their policyholders as the banks do about their customers, and sometimes more. If they engage to underwrite insurance, agents have to know what kind of moral risks are involved, and the insurance companies trust them to write policies for far larger amounts than money loaned on a car.

After my explanation, the leading Indianapolis banks agreed to extend a line of credit with us if we started a finance company for insurance agents. We talked to the Board of Directors of the insurance company, and they too were enthusiastic and even offered to buy stock. Dudley sold all the stock necessary to launch the new company, which was not too difficult in the light of our record. We organized the Agents Finance Company, the first of its kind, in May, 1936. I was then thirty-four, and I was given complete responsibility for putting the company together and managing its operations.

By this time I had learned some of the principles of being an executive, one of which is to surround yourself with capable men. I had heard of a highly successful executive who had a two-word slogan: "Buy Brains." While this approach seemed materialistic and overly simple, it did have a point. One does have to have top men to have a top team. I looked for men with outstanding records at successful companies whose futures were temporarily stymied because of the seniority system. I always tried to conduct the interviews with empathy and understanding, to enter into the other person's world and find out what he was looking for.

In seeking a manager for our finance company, it seemed to me the place to start was GMAC, General Motors Finance Company, since they had an excellent performance record and because their personnel had been hand-picked and trained. I wanted a man who had all the answers to all the problems of loaning money on automobiles. Fortunately I located such a man, an assistant manager of a large GMAC branch who supervised credit on millions of dollars of finance business. With him as a nucleus, we secured several other men from GMAC and two from another large finance company. With this team, plus a good sales organization, we soon had hundreds of our agents financing cars.

The plan continued to grow in popularity, and we made it available to agents of all insurance companies. This didn't hurt the American States agents, for the other agents had their own clientele, and it only meant that they secured this business instead of losing it to a dealer finance company.

Our insurance business continued to grow and prosper, and I began to think of other states to which we might expand. It may seem strange, because of its distance from Indianapolis, but the state I chose to consider entering was California, and there were many valid reasons for doing so. First, there were more automobiles in Los Angeles County than in the entire state of Indiana. Secondly, since it was fast-growing territory, the agents did not have deep roots with old, established, eastern companies, and this made them open-minded. They were more interested in present product and future possibilities than in past size and prestige. I secured some of this information from our reinsurance companies operating there and from friendly competitors with offices on the West Coast. And in 1938 I made a preliminary trip to survey the situation.

In order to open a branch office so far from Indianapolis, we needed three men: a sales manager, an underwriter to underwrite risks, and a claims manager. I interviewed a number of people, found three top men for these jobs, and advised them that I would confirm our arrangement after clearing it with our Board of Directors.

On this trip I got in touch with my old friend Dick Powell, and he invited me to lunch at Warner Brothers, where he was making a picture. He was extremely cordial and seemed happy to see me. Success had not changed him; he was as warm and good-natured as ever. A few days later he invited me to the best party I have ever attended. It was the first Annual Tri-Guild Ball of Actors, Directors, and Writers and was held at the Ambassador Hotel, where I was staying. Dick was then married to Joan Blondell, and I attended the ball with them. As we entered, a girl from Indianapolis whom I knew well, and who was staying at the Ambassador with her aunt, saw me come in with this crowd of celebrities. When I saw her the next day, she said, "Good Lord, Ed, why should I come all the way to

California and stand in line to watch you go to a party?" It seemed that everybody in the movie industry was there, and they furnished their own entertainment, which included the songs and antics of Bob Burns, Judy Garland, Fanny Brice, Ethel Merman, Jack Benny, George Burns, Gracie Allen, Bill (Bojangles) Robinson, Edgar Bergen and Charlie McCarthy. Dick, of course, knew everybody and introduced me to a number of the celebrities. He later sent me the ball's program autographed by Bette Davis, James Cagney, Robert Taylor, Clark Gable, and others.

After I returned to Indianapolis, I secured the approval of my plans to enter into business in California, and in a few months we had our state license. I then returned to Los Angeles and secured a well-known sales manager, who had quite a wide acquaintance among insurance agents. With this advantage, he was soon able to appoint a number of good agents for the American States, and our underwriter and claims manager were well able to service the business.

Judging from my active life, it might appear that I had little time for Mother. Such, however, was not the case. I was out of town perhaps one-fourth of the time, and when I was in the city, I spent at least three or four nights a week with her. On one or two of these, we would go to the movies, which she enjoyed immensely. Other evenings we read, as she had always been an avid reader. She continued to have endless health problems; some involved accidents, others illness. By now she had developed hypertension, which occasionally caused severe headaches and dizzy spells. On two occasions her dizziness resulted in serious accidents. One occurred in the theater, where she fell and broke her ankle, another at home, where she fell over the railing on a stairway and crushed two vertebrae. Although I had a registered nurse with her at the time, the nurse had left her for a moment.

Mother also had some serious sinus infections and, on one occasion, pneumonia. She actually set up a climate for respiratory infection herself, without realizing it. Her high blood pressure probably accounted for her constant want of fresh air, and even on the coldest winter nights, she would insist on having her windows open. A nose and throat specialist advised her time and again to just turn down the heat at night and keep her windows closed, but in vain.

Her physical ailments accentuated her nervous problems, and I could see that she was getting suspicious of more people and beginning to suffer delusions. Once she refused to take medicine from her orthopedic doctor, insisting that it would make her sick because she was sure there was poison in it; however, she reluctantly told the doctor that she would take the medicine if he took some first. I am sure he realized that he was violating all the rules of medical practice by submitting to the test, but he was a good friend and did take some of the medicine first. By one of those quirks of fate, he got deathly sick to his stomach, and Mother did not.

I then consulted a leading internist about Mother's problems, and after examining her and finding no physical basis for some of her symptoms, he advised me to have her see a psychiatrist. After some resistance from Mother, I arranged for an appointment. The doctor spent about an hour with her on the first visit and said that he could not analyze her situation specifically without spending much more time with her, but that he did know she needed psychiatric help. I placed Mother on a regular schedule with him as soon as possible, but her condition soon deteriorated, and we arranged for her to go to St. Vincent's Hospital. They had no psychiatric section, but with full-time special nurses they could take good care of her. She stayed at the hospital for months, and I visited her every evening I was in town. The nurses always left the room when I was there, and quite often I read devotional material to her. Many, many nights I stayed past visiting hours until midnight or later. The Sisters were wonderful to both of us and arranged for me to have coffee or a sandwich at any hour.

I lack the words to describe the frustration, sorrow, and agony I went through with Mother. I don't think anyone can know the anguish of mental illness without experiencing it himself or with a loved one. I think that even a psychiatrist experiences it synthetically. He has the scientific knowledge to help, but it is something one can only truly feel by experience.

Certain types of mental suffering are so deep-rooted that all logical or rational approaches only produce frustration. Unfortunately, at this time, there were no available private-duty nurses who could understand this kind of paranoidal case. Mother had constant arguments with the nurses whenever they had to carry out the doctors' orders or follow any disciplinary measures. Under these conditions, the nurses wanted to quit, and Mother pleaded with me to replace them on grounds that they were working against her. Nurses came and went like people going through a revolving door. If the Sisters had not been so understanding and considerate, I am sure they would have asked me to transfer Mother to another hospital.

One evening after I left the hospital, I felt particularly lonely and depressed. When I got home I stayed up most of the night thinking about the vicissitudes of life.

Mother had been born into an ideal family, with an environment marked by love, faith in God, and financial security, living in one of the mansions of the day.

She appears to have been her father's favorite as he took her on many of the calls on his patients throughout the countryside with his horse and buggy; and he also permitted her the free use of his soda fountains in the drugstores he owned. An avid reader of good books, he got her interested in them at an early age. With this foundation she became extremely well read and could express herself beautifully. At Earlham College where she enrolled, she studied art under Professor Bundy, one of Indiana's leading artists, already famous for his paintings of beechwoods. Two of Mother's portraits, done in pastels at the age of fourteen, hung in our house. She also produced many watercolors and oils, and we had several of these too. She gave others to her family. All of this work was completed by the time she was a nineteen-year-old sophomore at Earlham College.

My mother's parents and all of her Quaker ancestors evidently had enjoyed responsible, successful, and reasonably tranquil lives. All had been farmers in Indiana for nearly a hundred years, with the exception of her father who became a doctor. With this ideal cultural climate, why didn't she wait and marry one of the many responsible, eligible men in Richmond, instead of walking into a buzzsaw with my father? This always baffled me, and on one occasion I asked my uncle, Charles Purcel, who had married my aunt, Myrtle Teague, to explain the mystery. He was a Richmond man, employed by the Pennsylvania Railroad, when my father was introduced to my mother at a party given by one of Father's customers. Uncle Charlie, it appeared, had also been astounded by Mother's choice of a husband, but his explanation for it was very simple. Mother had led a sheltered, protected life with a Quaker family in a small community. Father was handsome and better dressed than the local young men, had a magnetic personality, and talked glibly about Chicago and other large cities he had visited. Under the slim pretense of buying something at the drugstore, he also managed to display the largest roll of bills any of the local young folks had ever seen. He must have seemed to Mother the proverbial knight on a white horse.

Her parents advised against the marriage, but she was so infatuated that, reluctantly, they gave their permission, recognizing that Father's parents were responsible, respectable people in Indianapolis. And in all fairness to Father, he must have also loved her as much as he was capable of loving anyone.

Later I learned that Mother's days of bitter disillusionment began shortly after marriage. She and Father rented an Irvington house, several blocks from the streetcar line, with no other means of transportation available. Though the house was attractive and surrounded by trees, Mother was completely isolated except for her near neighbors. Father traveled a great deal, which was bad enough, but often he did not arrive home at the appointed hour. Mother told me that many times she prepared a lovely dinner and was looking forward to his return, only to have him arrive hours later on the verge of drunkenness, or not arrive at all. Often she had to go downtown to find him in a saloon and bring him home. It was like an old-fashioned melodrama of the last century, except this one was real. According to my aunt and uncle, she kept all of this trouble to herself, because she knew she had been wrong in marrying against her family's wishes, and she had too much pride to admit that she had made a terrible mistake.

After she had been married two years, Mother had a little

daughter, born dead, which was a terrible ordeal both mentally and physically. The delivery was made at home by a general practitioner. Shortly after this, her father died in a tragic accident in his drugstore. He was mixing something that contained alcohol, which caused a fire that ignited his beard, burning his face horribly.

As I reflected on these various circumstances late into the night, I asked myself why in the name of God such a terrible accident would befall my grandfather, who had been a paragon of virtue, why my mother had suffered the tortures of the damned, and why my father, who had come from prominent and responsible ancestors, had blemished the family name. I further mused that if they had not married, I would not have been born, and consequently, would not have been sitting around in my living room alone at three in the morning, drinking cup after cup of coffee and thinking these thoughts.

The whole damnable setup made no sense—the accident of being born at all, being what we are, beginning to die from the day we are born, millions of cells dying and being reborn daily, nature anticipating its own breakdown and destruction until the rebuilding process falls behind, and we die, unless some accident or other onslaught takes us sooner.

Finally, I said, "To Hell with it!" I would never understand life, anyway. I took a sleeping pill, went to bed and had bad dreams. The next day I determined not to brood over this morass of troubles and endeavored to arrive at a constructive course of action. At the office I was looking through *Fortune* magazine when I noticed an article about the Menninger Clinic at Topeka, Kansas. It was a beginning.

The piece gave a glowing account of accomplishments in the field of mental health. I was excited about it and talked to Dudley immediately, saying that this clinic looked like a ray of hope for Mother. He was always generous and cooperative in sharing the expenses of Mother's illness, though I was disappointed that he did not devote more time to her. Perhaps it was because he was such an extrovert and too impatient to spend hours in a hospital room. Our doctor wrote Menninger's and, though there was a waiting list, they replied that they probably could admit Mother in a month or so.

Shortly after receiving this information, I began to explore a way to tell Mother our plans. I knew the disclosure would be extremely difficult for her, since her attachment to me was so great that my visits had become her only pleasure. The Menninger Clinic had informed us that if they took Mother's case, they would not allow Dudley and me to visit her until they approved. I did not like this prerequisite, but because I was desperate to help Mother, and because everything in the past had failed, I felt that I had to take their advice. However, I did not tell Mother that I would be unable to visit her until the doctors agreed. In fact, I intimated that I would visit her frequently. I had never told Mother a lie in my life on a serious matter, and now I was put in the agonizing position of telling her a deliberate lie in order to give her the help she needed.

Mother trusted me with the innocent faith of a child, and this made my wound doubly deep. I read the article in *Fortune* to her and assured her that the doctors at Menninger's were kind, good people, which they certainly are. I also talked to Sister Andrea, the head of St. Vincent's Hospital, and she and the other Sisters reassured Mother, because they also thought the plan was for the best.

When departure day finally came, one of the private-duty nurses agreed to accompany Dudley, Mother, and me on the trip to Topeka. We had to leave early in the morning, and not only Sister Andrea but the whole upper echelon of Sisters from St. Vincent's accompanied us to the station and stayed with us until Mother was on the train. They were truly "angels of mercy" and an honor to their order. That morning was of such magnitude in my life that I can remember it in the most minute detail.

We arrived at Menninger's after a hectic trip, during which Mother was alternately numb and hysterical with fear. After we toured the grounds and buildings, Dudley and I were reassured, for the setting was more like a small college campus than a hospital. Mother's room was in a building that looked like a sorority house, and the nurse who received her was very attractive and cheerful.

We soon met both Dr. Karl and Dr. William Menninger, who intuitively sensed Dudley's feelings and mine. They did not attempt to make any predictions about Mother's case, merely assuring us that all of their resources would be at her disposal. They advised us to leave Mother immediately and to return to Indianapolis; otherwise, they could not properly treat her. It was one of the most tragic moments of my life when I said goodbye to her, for I could tell by the wounded look in her eyes that she knew I had lied to her. I felt like a traitor. I cursed myself and God that the price of helping her came so high. Mother loved flowers, and before we left, we did manage to arrange with the local florist to send her fresh-cut flowers every day.

When we returned from Menninger's, Dudley invited me to stay with him for a while, but I preferred to stay home alone with my housekeeper. I knew that I would feel lonely, but I would at least have the privacy of my own home and could always have friends or a date in for a candlelight dinner and a quiet evening talking and listening to mellow music. I had a record player that would play an assortment of records indefinitely, both in the living room and social room.

As soon as I returned, I began writing Mother every few days, and she, in turn, wrote me at least once a week for the first two months of her stay in Topeka. At first the letters were encouraging. She told me about her visits with Dr. Norman Reider, who had been assigned to her case, and about some of the little parties that were given for the patients. Then gradually her letters were less frequent and more despondent, and then there were no letters at all.

We had taken Mother to Menninger's in the fall of 1938, and as Christmas approached I wanted very much to see her. Dr. Reider advised against a visit, but added that if I should come, I should not do it during the holidays, for a visit at that time, he believed, would only increase Mother's anxiety. Therefore, I made my trip shortly after the first of the year. Mother had been transferred to what was known as the White Cottage, reserved for more disturbed patients, and she had a nice front room from which she could watch the highway traffic. I don't think there was ever a meeting between mother and son that was more highly charged with emotion. It was as though our personalities burst open and became one. I know she had taken great pains to prepare for our meeting by being as well groomed as possible, but there was a sad, tormented look in her eyes. At that moment I would have given my life to assume her suffering. A verse from *Macbeth* flickered in my mind:

> Can'st thou not minister to a mind diseased,
> Pluck from the memory a rooted sorrow,
> Raze out the hidden troubles of the brain
> And with some sweet oblivious antidote
> Cleanse the stuff'd bosom of that perilous stuff
> Which weighs upon the heart?[3]

The first day I was allotted only an hour's visit with Mother, and though I told her I could see her again before I left, I knew that she did not quite believe me. Our parting was terribly difficult. Afterward I visited with Drs. Norman Reider, Robert P. Knight, Karl Menninger, and William Menninger, all of whom were familiar with Mother's case. At that time this whole constellation of talent saw patients individually. Dr. Reider went on to an outstanding practice in California, Dr. Robert Knight became the head of the famous Austin Riggs Hospital in Stockbridge, Massachusetts, and the Menningers' record of course speaks for itself.

I had a long session with Dr. Will Menninger, who had the patience to explain Mother's problem and mine in layman's terms. The heart of the matter was that, as a sensitive, idealistic, protected person, Mother was ill-equipped for the disappointment and suffering she had encountered, and as her world got smaller and smaller, she had attached her life more completely to mine. Deep within, she knew it was neither right nor possible for me to devote my entire life to her, yet she could not face the reality of seeing me with others, particularly other women. I, too, was deeply involved, because I had a great love for her; but, unconsciously, this was mixed with resentment, because I did not have full adult freedom. Since I would not permit myself to admit the resentment, I repressed it subconsciously. This, in turn, produced deep guilt feelings that only added to my agony. Thus we were both trapped in misery, and though I could be helped by insight into my problem, it was almost impossible for her to gain the insight she needed, due to her age and her physical and mental condition. If, by some miracle, she could gain this insight, what would she do about it? How could she adjust her life and accept reality, find new values and goals?

Dr. Will Menninger's prognosis was not optimistic, yet there was little I could do about it. Mother was getting the best specialized care possible, and though it tore my heart to see her suffer, I felt it would only make matters worse to take her home. I could not be with her all the time, and she might hurt herself as she had before.

I had further talks with the doctors and asked each of them if they had any philosophical or theological answer to so much meaningless suffering, and I found myself questioning once more the ultimate meaning of life. The doctors said that their profession necessarily limited itself to the behavior of people during their life span, that they did not attempt to take a scientific position on philosophical or theological problems. Their business was to try to help people who were sick, and fortunately they were making a lot of progress in this field.

My second and last visit with Mother at this time was heartrending, and several times I was on the verge of taking her home, getting some nurses, and looking after her myself, in spite of professional opinion, my business, and other factors. I weighed this decision many times while I talked to her. Finally, my head ruled my heart.

I went on to California from Topeka and thought about Mother most of the time. I decided that, when I returned home, I would reread the entire Bible carefully and see if I could gain any new insight into the mysteries of life.

I began with the Old Testament, and my only reaction was negative. The "scientific" conclusions of the writers were childlike, I thought, while their ignorance and morals were deplorable. I was revolted by the hatred, cruelty, murder, fratricide, robbery, rape, incest, and slavery. It seemed preposterous for a man living about 1000 B.C. to look backward four billion years and give us an account of the creation of the earth.

Many of the miracles were clearly figments of someone's imagination, e.g: Daniel unharmed in the Lion's Den (Daniel 6: 16–24); and Joshua making the sun stand still (Joshua 10:12–14).

The ethics and morals of the Old Testament impressed me as those of a barbaric and vengeful people worshiping a barbaric and vengeful God, invading and conquering countries without provocation, confiscating property, murdering innocent victims or selling them into slavery. A sampling:

> A king sees another man's wife taking a bath and plots to send her husband, a soldier loyal to him, into battle and have him murdered (II Samuel 11:2–27).
>
> Two of Lot's daughters get him drunk so that they can have sexual intercourse with him (Genesis 19:30–38).
>
> A God employs she-bears to tear up small boys (II Kings 2:23, 24).
>
> King Ahab covets Naboth's vineyard and robs him of it by means of a rigged court (I Kings 21:1–16).
>
> Solomon is highly honored for self-indulgence with a harem of three hundred concubines and seven hundred wives (I Kings 11:3).
>
> A God is interested in men's slaughtering all manner of fowls and animals as a sacrifice and even sends one of the Chosen to undertake the murder of His own son to show his loyalty to Him—Abraham (Genesis 22:1–14).
>
> Women and children are murdered by divine command in the ruthless extermination of the Amalekites (I Samuel 15:3).
>
> Disasters befall men as the result of divine wrath (Genesis 19:24).

The only redeeming features I found in the Old Testament were in the Prophets and in some of the Psalms, but these gave me nothing to fortify my faith in God. They merely told me of men struggling for justice or comfort. It became clear to me that the claim of infallibility is irreconcilable with what this book contains.

Most of all, I was shocked by the general low ethical level which I found in the Hebrew Scripture. The supposed "good guys" stole with impunity. What right had the people of Israel to attack the Philistines and try to conquer their country? It seemed to me that the people who were glorified in the Bible were really the aggressors. Abraham's apparent presence there earlier could not justify the theft of land in a later generation. I was appalled that Jahweh seemed to condone aggression by some, while he criticized it by others. Where, then, could I find any support of moral consistency and fair dealing? In the end I tended to agree with Hendrik Van Loon:

> The Old Testament was a national Jewish scrap-book. It contained histories and legends and genealogies and love poems and psalms, classified and arranged and reclassified and rearranged without regard for chronological order or literary perfection.[4]

Reading the New Testament, I concluded that it presented a much higher conception of God, and that its ethical teachings were on a much higher level. However, I soon realized that the message was unduly mixed with miracles, which I could not accept as historical facts; in addition, many of the teachings, including the sayings of Christ, I found mutually contradictory.

My doubts about the miracles started with the report, in Matthew and Luke, of the virgin birth of Jesus. I soon saw that there was an apparent division of opinion on this point, even among the early Christians. Neither Mark nor John mentions Christ's birth at all, while Matthew and Luke, which report His birth from a virgin, include genealogies in which the ancestry is traced through Joseph. What point was there in tracing a person's ancestry through a man if he was not the earthly father? Then, many of the miracles attributed to Jesus bothered me, e.g.:

Walking on the water (Matthew 14:25–27).
Curing a man born blind (John 9:13–33).
Raising Lazarus from the dead after he had been entombed four days (John 11:1–44).

Finding a coin in the fish's mouth to pay the temple tax (Matthew 17:24–27).

Even more troublesome were the sayings and deeds of Christ, which seemed mutually inconsistent, such as:

The Sermon on the Mount compared to Christ's anger in the temple, when He overturned the tables and drove out money changers (Mark 11:15–17).

His saying, "I have not come to bring peace but a sword" (Matthew 10:34–38).

His not permitting a prospective follower to bury his father, saying harshly, "Let the dead bury the dead" (Luke 9:59–60).

The story of the Unjust Steward in which it appears that Christ was commending and therefore encouraging somewhat dishonest or at least sharp practice (Luke 16:1–9).

Worst of all was the parable of the Pounds. Here the character who seems to represent God is depicted as grasping and terribly cruel:

But as for these enemies of mine, who did not want me to reign over them, bring them here and slay them before me (Luke 19:27).

Another problem of acceptance I had with the New Testament concerned the literal existence of angels, demons, and Satan. Discussion of Satan and the demons seemed pure witchcraft to me, the angels like a fantasy out of *Alice in Wonderland*. A demon was literally driven out of the man who called it "legion," then entered a group of pigs, which went screaming over the edge of a precipice (Mark 5:1–13). I was worried both by the calm assumption that demons actually exist as objective beings and by Christ's bland unconcern for either the pigs or their owners. Other examples:

Satan actually tempted Christ (Matthew 4:1–11).

There were twelve legions of angels, who could be summoned at will (Matthew 26:53).

I liked the Beatitudes and their negative counterparts, but I found some of them confusing:

But woe unto you that are rich; you have received your consolation.
Woe unto you that are full for you shall be hungry.
Woe unto you that laugh now for you shall mourn and weep.

If we should apply these sayings literally, philanthropists would fall in all three categories, and most people doing good works would be in categories two and three. To me these three verses seemed irrelevant, having nothing to do with the moral state of a person.

I noticed that there were conflicting reports of events. The cleansing of the temple was reported as occurring both early and late in Christ's public career. There were conflicts in the account of the resurrection. According to Mark, one young man announced to the surprised visitors at the tomb that Jesus was risen; according to Luke, two men; according to Matthew, one angel; and, according to John, two angels. In Mark's account, the women coming from the tomb agreed to "say nothing to anyone"; while in Luke they tell all these things to the eleven and to all the rest. I realized that these inconsistencies did not bother devout believers, but they bothered *me*. I could not simply arrive at a facile solution and give up my inquiring spirit.

Fall, 1939. Mother's condition had continued to deteriorate. I still wrote her at least twice a week, and the flowers from the local florist continued to come to her every day. She had not written me for months, although Dr. Reider frequently apprised me of her condition. He and the staff had used every method known to them to help her, but her problems, physical and mental, were so serious and so deeply imbedded that the physicians were unable to do much for her. She had high blood pressure, and her mental worries had cut wounds too deep for even modern medical science to reach. I was told that Mother had now become so despondent that she had been placed in restraints and that the nurses had to resort to force-feeding; consequently, she had become emaciated

For a long time I had been debating bringing Mother home, and I finally decided to take this step. I advised Dudley that I could no longer bear to think of her suffering without me. If the best medical talent in the world could not make her well, at least I could take care of her, and this seemed more important to me than anything else. Since the Menningers did not hold out any hope for her recovery, they could understand my feelings, and they arranged for one of their special psychiatric nurses to accompany us home. When Dudley and I arrived at Mother's room, she couldn't believe her eyes, for she had evidently decided long ago that she would never see us again. I was horrified beyond description at her appearance. She seemed to have shrunk to an old woman, and her eyes and facial expression embodied all the torment and suffering of the ages. I shall never know how much Mother contributed initially to her illness by refusing to face reality, but whatever her faults they were minor compared to the penalty she was paying. It seemed to me that she had been sentenced to life imprisonment, when she should only have been reprimanded.

As we boarded the train for home, my feelings were a mixture of joy and sorrow—sorrow that she looked and felt so bad, and joy that she would spend the rest of her life with me. Joy and sorrow are strange but constant bedfellows, as Kahlil Gibran knew well:

> Some of you say, "Joy is greater than sorrow," and others say "Nay, sorrow is the greater."
> But I say unto you, they are inseparable.
> Together they come, and when one sits alone with you at your board, remember that the other is asleep upon your bed.
> Verily you are suspended like scales between your sorrow and your joy.[5]

As soon as we arrived home, I arranged for a housekeeper to prepare the foods that Mother liked best, and our family doctor prescribed the proper vitamins in case we could get Mother to take nourishment. I tried to have all my morning and evening meals with her, which had a positive effect, for she started eating again. I quit traveling at this time and stayed home with her

five or six nights a week. Her courage in trying to regain her
health was magnificent and made me ashamed of my own com-
plaining. She came home in a daze, but she was gradually coming
out of it—a miracle of the power of love and determination. Our
love for each other was achieving something that even the greatest psychiatrists could not create.

After a month or so, she was able to go for a drive, accompanied by the nurse. With this progress on the one hand, complications set in on the other. She wanted me to release the
special nurse who had been so helpful. I did my best to convince
her that this would be a mistake, for I thought her wish was
based on an irrational jealousy. In addition, this step would make
life much more difficult for me, since it gave me a sense of
security to have an expert with us who understood Mother's case.
In the end, however, I succumbed to her entreaties, because
I wanted to avoid all possible arguments. We then secured a
warm if not highly skilled practical nurse who, surprisingly enough,
worked out fairly well. She was patient and kind and seemed to
help Mother eventually, though nothing was ever accomplished
on schedule.

As time went on, Mother regained most of the thirty pounds
she had lost and even improved enough for me to take her to
a movie once or twice a week. On these occasions, I arranged
for a private dining room at one of the clubs for dinner before
the show. I was living up to what I had planned to do, making
her life my first priority and everything else secondary.

As we approached the Christmas season, she started making
rather elaborate plans for decorations. She not only wanted the
customary Christmas tree, wreath, and inside decorations, but an
arrangement of lights on most of the shrubbery. While I thought
this was unnecessary, I agreed to it anyway, purchasing hundreds
of feet of colored lights. As Christmas approached and the
workmen came, her excitement increased, and I sensed that she
was working herself up to a crisis. I could not reason with her
logically without hurting her feelings and once or twice I lost
my patience, a situation I had done my best to avoid. As bad
luck would have it, on one of these occasions I told her that

my interest in Christmas was in the spirit of it and not the superficial fanfare of decorations.

That evening after I had retired, the nurse called me frantically in the middle of the night, saying that Mother was very sick. I rushed to her room and immediately knew that something was seriously wrong. I reached our doctor at his home, and he came immediately. What I had feared for so long had happened: she had had a serious heart attack. The doctor thought it would be better not to move her and arranged for the delivery of an oxygen tent. The next two days she seemed to improve, but shortly after dinner on the second night, I got another urgent call from the nurse. Mother was having another severe attack. Again, I was able to get in touch with the doctor and Dudley immediately, but before they arrived she died. Alone with her and the nurse, I was numb with shock. Christmas was on Monday, and she had died the preceding Saturday night. After all her expectations she did not even get to see another Christmas. And the irony of it all—the house and grounds flooded with Christmas cheer and Mother dead inside.

Dudley and I arranged for the funeral to be held at my home. Besides the many other flowers, we ordered a blanket of roses, her favorite flowers. I was not a member of a church at that time, but I arranged for Dr. Wick, a Unitarian minister I had met, to conduct the services. We used two of her favorite verses: Tennyson's *Crossing the Bar* and, from the Bible, "In my Father's house are many mansions, if it were not so, I would have told you. . . ." She was placed in the family mausoleum that we had just constructed two years before. As I left the cemetery, I felt grief to the depths of my being.

"He was weeping," wrote Remy de Gourmont, "but the tears ran into his throat and not down his cheeks, and like one of Dante's damned souls, he swallowed an inexhaustible and poisoned stream of grief."

Four

Since I was miserable at home alone and, at the same time, did not want to be a guest at Dudley's I considered a trip to Los Angeles and Honolulu. I wanted to get as far as was possible from the scene of my suffering. Katie thought Dudley should also get away, so they were amenable to the trip. Within days the three of us were on our way. After stopping in Los Angeles for a few days to conduct some business and visit Uncle Ed, Jack, and Donald, then living in Hollywood, we boarded the *Matsonia* for the voyage to Hawaii.

Before leaving, one of my friends had suggested that I meet a certain girl on the ship who was on her way to Honolulu to visit friends. He had told her that I might look her up and introduce myself. After the first two nights out, I still didn't feel like meeting anyone, but I decided to get in touch with the girl anyway and found her a very attractive and friendly brunette. I invited her to a dinner dance, where we were joined by Katie and Dudley. I then saw her the following day, made another date for dinner, and arranged to pick her up at her stateroom.

That evening when I knocked on the door, she asked me to come in, and it was like a charge of electricity. She had on a transparent, red silk robe that clung to her like gossamer, disclosing every detail of her body. The scent of perfume filled the room, and she radiated sex like a heat wave. I thought "My God, at a time like this!" The situation was perfect for a bachelor, but the timing was bad. I was in no mood then for even a Cleopatra. She must have thought I was the most stupid of men when I excused myself so that she could dress. When I returned later after my hasty exit, she was still agreeable and we had a most pleasant evening with Katie and Dudley.

At Waikiki, we stayed at the Royal Hawaiian Hotel, and the service was superb. There always seemed to be a waiter or an attendant on hand to anticipate our every wish. Again, the setting was perfect, but the timing was bad; I simply couldn't enjoy the beauty around me as I might have normally.

As the days wore on, I spent a lot of time on the beach and finally overexposed myself. A bad case of sunburn resulted in chills and fever. I had to stay in my room for two days, and at this time my thoughts turned to a girl I had been seeing a lot of lately.

When I was twelve years old and Mother was getting her divorce, there was born in Indianapolis a girl destined to have a great influence on my life. I first met Dorothy Fitzpatrick in 1937 in New York, where she was sharing an apartment with two other Indianapolis girls. Having been a model at L. S. Ayres in Indianapolis, Dorothy was doing modeling and sales work in Manhattan. A few months after I met her, she returned home and I began dating her. At 120 pounds, five feet three, she was a well-formed bundle of energy. She had a slightly round face with brown hair, dark brown eyes, and clear white skin. She also had a sparkling, radiant personality, unbounded enthusiasm, and an intuitive, practical, follow-your-heart philosophy which was a refreshing contrast to my often pensive, moody disposition. She brought sunshine into my life, she was a pleasure to be with, and she was good for me.

It was a new experience for me to be lonesome for a girl. Since I could not see her personally until I returned from Hawaii, I picked up the telephone and called her. It was about dinner-time in Indianapolis. I was glad to hear her cheerful voice, and I must have talked a long time, for she mentioned that I was as casual as if I were calling locally. Whatever the cost of the call, it was worth it, because I felt much better afterward.

As we left for home, Dudley, Katie, and I took one last look at Honolulu. It was a jewel of a city, on the southeast shore of Oahu, itself a paradise of exotic birds, beautiful flowers and foliage, with panoramic views of mountains and valleys surrounded by the clear green water of the sea and nourished by a soft, mild climate.

It was now January, 1940, and the war in Europe had been going on for one and a half years. So far it had not involved the United States directly, but we were reminded of it as warships and airplanes went out and returned at the same time each day. On Saturday night, everyone was always in a holiday mood and going to a party. It seemed to me that the whole setup was too mechanical and pat. Foreign powers needed no undercover agents to sense what was going on, because the pattern was deeply set for any observers. Still, little did we know, when we boarded this ship, of the tragedy that lay ahead for this beautiful, sunny city.

When we got off the train at the little neighborhood station in north Indianapolis, it was one of the coldest days on record, about twenty degrees below zero with more than a foot of snow on the ground. Dorothy was there to meet us, and the warmth of her smile and personality was in direct contrast to the temperature. After Dudley and Katie left us, I took Dorothy home. After a visit with her over a steaming cup of coffee, I went to my house, where I was met by my housekeeper and experienced wildly mixed feelings. The house was immaculate and beautiful, but I was struck by the joy and sorrow of it all, by the meaning of aloneness.

The next morning after breakfast, I spent an hour or so meditating before I went to the office. Since I had been gone for more than a month, I knew my desk would be loaded with stacks of mail and year-end reports waiting to be reviewed. Though I was still in a fog about some matters, there was one thing I was certain of: I could pour myself into business. Intensive work was constructive and profitable to me and to our personnel and stockholders; furthermore, keeping mentally occupied was good therapy. I soon got deeply involved with plans for new growth. I decided that we should expand our business to include all other lines of fire and casualty insurance.

Our company was now large enough to offer security and, at the same time, an opportunity for a person to get ahead fast.

Instead of being merely a small cog in a big machine, each talented man had a chance to be a key officer with us. Conducting the interviews was enlightening. About two out of every three applicants chose to remain where they were because of their tenure; they felt it gave them added security, including fringe benefits, which their family responsibilities seemed to require. They evidently agreed with some of my friends with larger companies who frequently cautioned me, when we continued to expand, that "little ships should stay close to shore." They did not seem to realize, when they gave me this pseudo-sage advice, that if Columbus had felt this way, he would never have discovered America.

However, the idea of coming with us appealed to the most venturesome and ambitious men we interviewed, who had confidence in themselves, and these were the only men I wanted anyway. They knew what Dudley and I had achieved from scratch and that we had carried an A-plus rating for management for years in the Alfred M. Best financial reports. I succeeded in recruiting several top men for the new insurance lines. In turn, I started on an educational project of my own, studying new lines of insurance, composing and editing the new policies and advertising materials. Many executives seemed to operate successfully without an intimate knowledge of each of their products, but I always felt I should have a working knowledge of every line we sold.

After the necessary printed forms and advertising materials were ready, we presented them to hundreds of agents in seven states. As always, we started a pilot project in Indiana. This called for a series of district sales meetings. Everyone who has launched the sale of new merchandise or products knows of the two-phase cycle: first, there is the scientific, analytical creation of the product conducted in an intellectual atmosphere; secondly, and in direct contrast, there is the presentation of the product in sales meetings, with an encore of entertainment and ballyhoo. Our sales meetings were a combination of decorous university classroom and lively entertainment, which always included cocktails, a good dinner, music, and an opportunity for more drinks and music afterward.

In Indiana we climaxed our district sales meetings with a state meeting, held at the Lake Wawasee Hotel. I arranged to rent the entire hotel before it closed for the season just after Labor Day. While there have been bigger and more expensive parties, I don't know of any as unusual or successful. When we registered our guests, we gave them a round of tickets which included payment for everything they might want to do. Besides the drinks and meals that were served at regular times, the tickets were good for anything between meals—tobacco, drinks, food, boat rides, fishing, and golf, including golf balls, caddies, clubs or even a golfing sweater if it was desired. We also had prizes for every game or sport from bridge to fishing.

We conducted the meetings in the mornings, leaving the afternoons and evenings free so that our agents could join various activities or just loaf. The second evening, I noticed that the crowd in the lobby was much smaller than usual, and I asked one of the waiters where the missing people were. He told me "confidentially" that there was a good-sized crowd in the gambling casino. I said I thought that the casino was closed, that the professional gamblers had gone. He said that this was true, but that the equipment was still there and that my favorite waiter, Burnsides, had opened the casino at the request of one of the agents who had visited it during the regular season. I thought, "For Christ's sake, what is Burnsides up to now?"

As I entered the casino, the sight was something to behold. Burnsides was running it at full-tilt for about fifty agents. He was acting as croupier at the crap table, and he had one waiter at the roulette wheel and another at the birdcage. The waiters were not banking the game but were taking small tips from agents, some of whom were banking the roulette wheel and birdcage. At the crap table, they were just shooting among themselves, and Burnsides was having a field day calling out numbers and bringing the dice back for the players. He had taken down an old curtain rod and bent the end to rake in the dice, and he added a little professional flavor by using well-known crap game lingo: No Game Rain, Little Joe, Big Dick, Boxcars, Snake Eyes, Eighter from Decatur, Ten the Hard Way, Seven Away the Line to Pay. He was using buttons off his jacket as markers for the side bets.

I had a very democratic relationship with our personnel and

agents. They had all the necessary respect for me to conduct business, but we also had a camaraderie which I would not have changed for anything. Pure business protocol never appealed to me and never will. As I surveyed the room and was invited by several agents to participate, I was in a somewhat delicate position. I didn't want to stop the game and spoil the fun, yet I didn't want it to go on indefinitely. On the spur of the moment I conceived a compromise that soon solved the problem. I announced that we would have to turn off the game in thirty minutes, since we were going to award the day's prizes in the main lobby. Fortunately, the game closed on time, and I didn't have to put a damper on the party. Walking back from the casino, I had a little talk with Burnsides. He looked at me with big, innocent eyes and said, "You know, boss, I was just trying to look after your guests." I know I was prejudiced in his favor, for he impressed me as quite a character.

Before I left to conduct the sales meeting at the lake, I had made arrangements with four friends to enroll in an evening course in philosophy at Indiana University Extension. My friends had all taken philosophy in college, but liked the subject so well that they wanted to continue work in the field. By this time, I had read quite a little philosophy myself. Will Durant's *The Story of Philosophy* had been very useful to me both as a bird's-eye view and as a stimulus to read the philosophers themselves.

In the intervening years, I had dipped into Plato and Aristotle, Bacon, Spinoza, Voltaire, Rousseau, Kant, Locke, and Hegel, though I probably spent more time with the nineteenth-century group: Schopenhauer, Nietzsche, Spencer, Russell, and William James. Since I had no instruction in this reading, I doubt if I absorbed all the significant points. But even on my own, I was intrigued. Every historic Western philosophy was, each in its own way, concerned with the purpose of life and the ultimate meaning of man, as was I.

All five of us remained with the course two years. Our teacher, William Jellama, professor of philosophy, was from the Bloomington campus of Indiana University. We were impressed both with his clarity and his power of illustration. Through his imaginative use of figures and similes, he was often able to get an idea across to me that I had missed in the more abstract areas. Although business trips out of the city sometimes prevented my attending classes, I managed never to fall behind in my reading.

The great additional benefit was the informal seminar set up by my four friends and me. After class we usually went to one of our homes for a bull session, which began with the material of the evening, but might move unpredictably from then on. I did my share of the talking and felt at ease with our group.

For a long time it seemed to me that the preoccupation of the Western philosophic tradition with the problem of *how we know* meant that its answer to life's meaning was a rationalistic one, *i.e.*, meaning lies in our knowledge. But when I considered the many theories of knowing—idealistic, realistic, empirical, rationalistic, etc.—I wondered if the philosophers of the West did not actually have more in common than their different theories might suggest. From Plato to Whitehead, were they not approaching the question of knowledge as man's instrument for finding meaning in his life, rather than as something separate?

I was then, as I am now, an amateur in philosophy, but I saw that most Western philosophy, no matter how erudite or abstract, was pointing ultimately toward practical questions of living. Also I saw that the intellectualism of Western philosophy often conceals its true concern from those who read too little or too rapidly. In addition, I saw that philosophy always involves perspectives, with their truths and their limitations, and that these perspectives pertain not only to the philosopher but to the age in which he lives; and therefore philosophy must be rethought and rewritten by many people in each generation. Eternal truths may be found in any competent philosophy; but there is no "eternal philosophy" impervious to change in the succeeding generation.

As for modern philosophies, I am familiar with the process thought of Whitehead, with logical positivism, and with existentialism. The central point of Whitehead's thinking is that the substantive categories of all Western thought through the nineteenth century need to be altered in the direction of a process view of all events.

As I understand it, logical positivism is concerned with positive facts and phenomena and tends to limit knowledge to what is known scientifically.

I have read most about modern existentialism; and I must agree that it is as hard to define as a flavor or an odor. Beginning with Kierkegaard in the middle of the previous century, existentialism seems to be an attempt to return to the immediacies of *human* existence. It has been suspicious of the rationalizing and abstracting tendencies of philosophies which, in their preoccupation with knowledge and reason and bare facts, seem to ignore the personal experiences of life. Kierkegaard argued with the rationalistic system of Hegel. Modern existentialists begin with anxiety, or the confrontation of death, or with love and sex, or with pain, suffering, sorrow, and guilt. These, they contend, are what *life* is about. Philosophy, the existentialists either assume or contend, is about life's meaning, not just about what man knows or what he can manipulate among the forces of nature. It is this emphasis that drew me to existentialism; for in the questions I asked, I had always been some kind of existentialist. I knew I had to look at life, draw my own conclusions, and finally die my own death. I was ready for the stress on individual responsibility that characterizes existentialism long before I ever heard the word. I discovered that existentialism's emphasis on the involvement of our lives with one another was also in keeping with my own thought. No man is either an island or a hermit. Man is man not simply because he has a mind, an instrument that can sort out general truths from a welter of concrete detail. He is a man because, whether he wants them or not, he has memory and imagination; he can "feel" himself in another place or time even when he is "here"; he is always confronted with choice, be it curse or blessing.

Although existentialist thinkers can be as far apart as Sartre, the atheist, and Marcel, the Christian, existentialism appealed to me because its questions are my questions, and its concerns are my concerns. I have strongly felt that in my own search for meaning, this was at least the right approach.

During this period my personal life was a rat race, full of activity and unresolved conflicts. Contemporary psychiatry recognizes the turmoil that is often caused within by the conflicting interests of the id, the ego, and the superego. The id being the unconscious, primitive, selfish, motivating force of our emotions; the ego being the intellectual, integrative powerful driving force of achievement; and the superego being the conscience that sits in moral judgment. These are general categories and not neatly separated since each impinges on the other, on the conscious, subconscious, and unconscious levels. However, it is well known that man has this trilogy of being, and the id, the ego, and the superego must live in some adjustment and harmony in man or he will be crucified by internal strife.

It is surprising how some geniuses of the past had a depth of insight to sense the inner turmoil that often rages in man. Long before Freud and modern psychiatry, it was aptly described by Shakespeare:

> . . . and the state of man,
> Like to a little kingdom, suffers then
> The Nature of an insurrection.

The great writer Dostoyevsky, whose life was a volcano of eruptions, was painfully aware of the trilogy of man in himself, which he dramatized so effectively in his masterpiece, *The Brothers Karamazov;* the id, personified by Dmitri, the man of passion; the ego, by Ivan, the intellectual; and the superego, by Alyosha, the man of religion.

My own personality was now torn with internal strife which came to life in disturbing dreams. At this point, I felt the impact of another verse from Shakespeare:

O God, I could be bounded in a nut-shell and count myself
a king of infinite space, were it not that I have bad dreams.[6]

In fact, I got interested in dreams and read some of the works of Dr. Carl Jung, the great Swiss psychiatrist.

It was perhaps the virulence of my own dreams at that time which made me interested in Jung's theory of the "collective unconscious." I had known that dreams were used as raw material in psychoanalysis, but it was the acquaintance with Jung that led me to think of the unconscious life as a reservoir of primitive feelings, symbols, and archetypical images reaching back to the dawn of human history.

Jung helped me to see that dreams are powerful evidences of the influence of the unconscious mind upon the actual life and thought of any human being. When a dream is going on, everyone knows that everything else, including reason, is "blacked out." I knew my dreams were trying to tell me something, but I was in no position to know precisely what, because they were wrapped in so many symbols, archetypes, and disguises. On this occasion I did not feel like going to a psychiatrist to interpret my dreams, although I did do just that years later and gained valuable insight.

From my observations and experience, I adopted a dualistic philosophy, which seemed to apply to everything in man, in nature, and in the universe—conscious and unconscious, good and evil, light and darkness, love and hate, the will to build and the will to destroy. Nature will take thousands of years building some work of grandeur and then destroy it in an instant through an earthquake, tidal wave, or some other irresistible force. Nature has helped to support and nourish man on his ascent from the lower animals and out of the caves, and then by a violent act it destroys him by the tens of thousands or wipes him out wholesale in an epidemic. Nature produces friendly bacteria to help keep men alive and unfriendly bacteria to destroy them.

Pharmaceutical houses specialize in germ warfare. The wonder drugs called antibiotics are a chemical substance produced by microorganisms which destroy or inhibit the growth of harmful bacteria or other microorganisms. In the universe, stars that took billions of years to form explode instantaneously; and our planet earth, which is at least four billion years old, will someday be a lifeless cinder.

If I did not have a strong will to believe, as well as to doubt, I might have just settled matters by becoming an atheist with Schopenhauer. "What is life on the largest scale," he asks, "but the same recurrent inanities, the same dog barking, the same fly buzzing forevermore?"

Instead, I arrived at the only acceptable philosophy for me, belief in a powerful, compassionate God who had an evil adversary of cosmic proportions to overcome.

In addition to my dedication to business and interest in philosophy, I found that I was falling in love with Dorothy and had reason to believe that she was in love with me. Instead of accepting this situation with gratitude, I went through a state of fighting love. I had carried such a heavy burden of responsibility, both at home and in business, that I rebelled against the added responsibilities of marriage and probable parenthood. Moreover, I had been a bachelor so long, with complete personal freedom, that I had no idea whether or not I could adjust to the stability of marriage. I had seen the problems of marriage in my own family, both in Mother's and Dudley's, and I felt that if I did marry, it would not be a halfway measure but a total commitment to making it a lifelong joyful experience. At this point, I do not know how much of the marriage barrier was my own selfishness and how much was simply concern for Dorothy's happiness, but often I would try to put off thinking about it by seeking distraction in social activities.

When the show *Hellzapoppin* was in town, a friend arranged a date for both of us with two very attractive actresses. After the show, we had supper at my home, which included champagne and crepes suzette. When I was in Honolulu, the hotel had used a beautiful silver chafing dish with an alcohol burner and silver skillet for crepes suzette, and I had ordered a similar one from Milan, Italy, which we used on this occasion.

My date was Lizabeth Scott who afterward went on to stardom in motion pictures. It was a most joyful evening, and the next day she presented me with a photograph inscribed "To Ed, the Host of Perfection."

On another occasion, a friend and I entertained two of the male leads from Maurice Evans's *Hamlet*. This was an equally vivid evening in a different way. It included a discussion of the theater and of Shakespeare, and of whether or not he really wrote the plays. The actors believed that he did because, for one thing, whoever wrote them had to have an intimate knowledge of the theater, and Shakespeare had this knowledge. As they put it, the plays really smelled of the theater. On the other hand, many critics disagreed with them, and they recommended to me one of the books presenting the opposite point of view, *Francis Bacon and His Secret Society*. I bought the book immediately, but after reading it and those of some of the other critics, I decided that the subject was too involved for me to arrive at an intelligent opinion, other than that whoever wrote the plays was the greatest literary genius of all time.

Just as we were breaking up, after several drinks and an enjoyable evening, the actor who played Laertes mentioned an interesting sidelight about the evening's performance and asked if I had noticed it. At the height of the duel between Hamlet and Laertes, Maurice Evans, playing Hamlet, whispered, "Hey, turn around and face the audience; your shirttail is coming out." (But I hadn't noticed.)

Some time later, I hosted a theatrical group on a larger scale. One evening when I was having dinner at the Athletic Club with Dorothy and two of my bachelor friends, another bachelor I knew, not a Bachelors' Club member, came into the dining room with two stunning girls. I made some excuse to ask him where in the world he had found them. He said, "Why, Ed, I have a whole show full of them." George White's *Scandals* was in town, and my friend knew some members of the cast, including Ben Blue, the star of the show. I invited him and his friends to join us at our table. One of the girls sat next to me, and Dorothy sat on my other side. I guess I got into too much animated conversation with the girl next to me to suit Dorothy, for after they all returned from the ladies' room, the girl who had been next to me sat down at the other side of the table.

By this time, I had had two or three drinks, and I asked my friend to invite the cast out to my house for a party after the show. He asked very matter-of-factly if I would like to have the jugglers too. I said, "Sure, bring out the entire show. Just let me know so that I can get a crew of waiters and inform my housekeeper." He called me a little later from the theater to say that the invitation had been accepted. I then sent word that I would have taxicabs waiting at the stage door to bring the party out. As I remember, it took an even dozen cabs to transport the cast.

Though the show was well worth the price of admission, we had a much better show of our own at my home. Ben Blue was an excellent comedian and even more amusing offstage. The cast seemed to have a real affection for him, and he, in turn, was warm and friendly and entered fully into the spirit of the party. His wife was traveling with him, and they gave an enthralling performance of mind reading. Though I watched closely, I never understood how they did it. His wife would leave the social room and go upstairs, and we would think up all manner of things, and when she returned she always had the answer. The jugglers brought only some of their props, balls which they could throw anywhere in the room which would always bounce back into their hands.

After these opening ceremonies, the party moved into high gear. Dorothy, my two bachelor friends, and I joined in a La Conga chain, the vogue at the time. The cast was talented enough to add a little zest to the dance, and one of my bachelor friends, who was a little overweight, rolled up his shirt Bikini-like, leaving his stomach bare. He stood on the sidelines, and as the girls went by, they would give his bare belly a friendly pat.

After a few drinks, the girls began to spread out all over the house, and I thought I had better take a moment to see what was going on. Some felt the urge, which often goes with alcohol, to call up their friends long-distance. I found two of them in my bedroom talking to someone in California. Since it seemed inappropriate to interrupt, I just left them alone and charged the call up to experience. There was a larger group in the kitchen with my housekeeper sampling various snacks and, in the living room, there was a girl quietly sipping a drink on the floor in front of my record machine, listening to Maurice Evans's Shakespeare records. She had asked me previously if I had any of his records, and after I showed her how to operate the machine, she seemed entirely contented. Later in the week I spent a quiet afternoon with her, driving through the countryside, talking about acting and plays. Though I had no knowledge of the theater, we had a delightful afternoon together. She must have enjoyed it too, for she sent me an autographed picture with the note: "May there be more days like this!"

The party went on and on, and I must say I enjoyed it as much as anyone. When I awoke the next morning, however, I had one of the worst hangovers of my life. I was reminded of an old story. It seemed that a very conservative gentleman wanted to purchase a parrot, but found that the bird used some profanity. The owner gave him instructions about how he could remedy this. He said that, should the parrot swear after he got him home, he was to take him out of the cage and whirl him around a few times by the neck and then throw him back in. Soon after the new owner took the parrot home, the bird exploded in profanity. The owner did as instructed, got him out of the cage, twirled him around violently, and threw him back in; whereupon, the parrot shook himself, blinked his eyes, and said, "Christ, what a breeze!"

Five

December 7, 1941. I was conducting a sales meeting at the Indianapolis Athletic Club when news came about Pearl Harbor. I could not have been more shocked if Japanese troops had invaded the Club. The news seemed too fantastic to be true. After the reports continued to pour in, I adjourned the meeting so that the men could return home, for I know that each person wants to be with his family in any crisis.

It is difficult to describe the management problems brought on by the war. Our female personnel left in droves, single girls got married, married ones had babies, others went into war plants at higher wages.

We would gladly have raised salaries to meet any competition, but we had to apply to the government for permission, and by the time permission was given, the birds had flown.

The war took an extra heavy toll of our male personnel, since our average age bracket was much lower than that of most companies. We lost most of our lower management men, many in the middle-management group, and a large number from the top. Within a year, our trained personnel were cut more than 50 percent. I realized that our problems were nothing compared to those of the men in military service, but it was terribly frustrating to operate efficiently when our replacement personnel constituted any help we could get.

Other insurance companies were having their personnel problems too, and for one of them, the problem was especially acute, since the person who owned 90 percent of the stock was neither active in the business nor able to take charge himself. Due to these circumstances, I got a tip that the Union Insurance Company might be for sale. Though it was a profitable company, the amount we could pay for it would provide more money for its stockholders than would present earnings, and at the same time we could make it very profitable for American States by consolidating departments and reducing overhead. Yet on the surface, it appeared foolish to consider buying another company when we had so many of our own management problems.

Another problem was that I was now forty and soon would be subject to induction into the army if I passed my physical. Many of my friends had secured commissions in the navy, and I should have preferred this service. However, several months earlier, a navy doctor had given me an unofficial examination and told me I would not pass my physical because of some broken veins in my left ankle, which I had injured years before in the interurban accident. After weighing matters carefully, I decided that I probably would be turned down by the army too, and in any event it was worth taking the chance that I would be on hand to manage the firm. Once again, the situation was one involving timing and alternatives. It was certainly not the season to buy, yet if the company were sold and we did not buy it, we should have lost our opportunity.

I talked over the matter with Dudley, who was not enthusiastic about buying. The Board of Directors was even less so, but supported my idea because of our performance record in the past. I then called on Dwight Peterson, president of an investment house that was associated with Pierre Goodrich, the principal owner of the Union Insurance Company. Our attorney, Kurt Pantzer, and Pierre Goodrich had gone to Harvard Law School together, which helped make it easy for Dudley and me to get acquainted with Pierre at our first meeting.

We four made an interesting study in personalities. Kurt Pantzer was a high-strung, talented, efficient lawyer with a large practice that filled his time; thus he liked to get to the heart of a matter quickly. Dudley was an extrovert who also liked to move directly to the business at hand. Pierre was an intellectual who was active behind the scenes in the ownership and management of many enterprises. I sensed that he liked to visit, spar around, and feel out a situation before entering into negotiations. I too liked to analyze and reflect on a proposition before making a major decision, but after it was made, I liked to move swiftly.

In our first visit with Pierre, I could tell that it would take a great deal of time and patience to come to an agreement, but the process was worthwhile as far as I was concerned, because the Union Insurance Company would mesh perfectly with our operations. The upshot of the preliminary negotiations was that Dudley and Kurt became discouraged after the second meeting and told me I would be foolish to pursue the matter. I said that I intended to go ahead regardless of time, since I knew in my heart that it was a good proposition for both Pierre and American States, and that we could both profit by it.

Pierre was a very gracious person, and if he wanted to take up part of our meeting talking about Greek philosophy and Asiatic mysticism, it was all right with me; for I had some knowledge of these subjects and would at least find them interesting. He was a highly intelligent person who simply approached matters differently from most businessmen. Instead of moving directly from "A" to "B," he chose to surround a subject in concentric circles. While his method took longer, it was effective in covering every item. Finally, after several months, Pierre and I arrived at the basis for a sale.

During these negotiations, I followed a code that I had already used effectively:

First, many things in life are matters of compromise, a choice of alternatives.

Second, in compromising, try to be as liberal as possible, give away the Kings but keep the Aces.

Third, keep in mind that you can afford to lose a few battles if you win the war.

I cannot overemphasize the important part these simple rules played in my life. I have seen many important transactions fall flat because both sides were too selfish and wanted a clean victory, which was impossible, or because of some sophomore who couldn't see the forest for the trees and wound up with a lot of petty victories, but lost the big one.

I wanted the Union Insurance Company even if I had to buy it myself. I was aware that I had a motivation besides profit (although the purchase turned out to be even more profitable than my projection); it gave me extra ego-satisfaction to buy the company for which I had started working at fifty dollars a month.

Another important business matter took place shortly after we bought the Union. Our automobile insurance volume was down, because no new cars were being manufactured, and I took a long look into the future. First, I had to assume that we were going to win the war and that, after this sad interruption, the United States would continue to grow and prosper. Thus, it seemed best for Dudley and me as well as the stockholders if we entered into a long-term management contract, whereby we would freeze our salaries for all future time and secure a bonus on increased volume tied into a profit formula. In other words, no bonus would be available except as a portion of increased profit. Eventually, this contract created more income for Dudley and me and was very profitable for the stockholders.

In the fall of 1942, I received notice to report for my army physical. A friend, formerly with a Chicago insurance company, had secured a navy commission and was now Lieutenant Commander in Charge of Officer Recruitment in the Indianapolis District. He and some other friends arranged a party for me the night before I was to be inducted (if I passed my physical). I had some other friends who had also received commissions, and since they all claimed that the army would take anybody who could walk, they addressed me as "Private Gallahue" all evening. I had outranked them in business, and they were having a lot of fun with the idea that they would soon outrank me in the military. I drank too much, and when I finally got to bed late that night, one of these jokers called to say it was time to report for duty. I told him to go to Hell, and then with a pair of scissors cut the telephone line in my bedroom.

It seemed that I had hardly closed my eyes when my housekeeper awakened me, and I was on my way to an old armory for my physical. At that time, the draft age limit was still forty-five. It was a sight to see the place filled with near-naked men going through a line like a flock of sheep. Many were so out of shape that I doubt they could have fought their way out of a paper bag. The doctors made entries on each person's examination form as the various tests were conducted, and I noticed that, at the end of the line, the men who were inducted turned one way, the 4-F's another. I couldn't help wondering which fork in the road I might take. Finally my turn came at the end of the line, and, after the doctor looked over the form and made a big check mark on one item, he told me that I was classified 4-F. I thought about what a Hell of a difference that little check mark made. Without it I would have wound up as a private on some clerical job, because of my physical impairment, instead of running an insurance company.

After I was classified 4-F, I made a very comprehensive survey of our business and streamlined it as much as possible. I did a large part of the work at home alone in the evening, and sometimes for diversion I listened to music or browsed through my books. Once I decided to examine the Gallahue family Bibles, some family letters, and old newspaper articles. I had not looked over this material for a long time, and for some reason the family records took on new interest. Soon I was reflecting on my ancestors' lives and the periods in which they lived.

There was a letter dated May 1, 1865, written by my great-uncle, Evender Kennedy, who had graduated in 1860 from De-Pauw University, then known as Asbury College, and enlisted in the Union forces from Muncie, Indiana. He later became a doctor, poet, and novelist. The letter was written to his mother from Appomattox Court House, where he witnessed Lee's surrender: "I am proud that I was present to see every detail of the surrender. . . . While victory inspired every heart with hope, came the news of the tragic death of our noble President. The shout was hushed, the cannon silenced—Every heart felt the blow. Every face was sad—you cannot believe with what reverence and love was held the name of Abraham Lincoln."

A letter marked June 20, 1853, West Union, Virginia, was from my great-grandfather Gallahue to my grandfather and his brother, both of whom came to Muncie, Indiana, at ages ten and twelve to live with relatives after their mother died. (Their father died shortly after the letter was written in a typhoid fever epidemic that wiped out almost the entire Gallahue family in Virginia.) His tone was quite solemn: "Be good and agreeable scholars. Read the Bible and always keep before your eyes that you are born to die and your conduct alone will bring you to meet your mother that is now in Heaven."

There was also a feature article from the Indianapolis *News*, December 26, 1929, about my great-grandfather, Andrew Kennedy, who was elected to Congress at age thirty and served three terms to 1846: "He declined nomination for a fourth term and came to Indianapolis and entered into the Senatorial canvass before the General Assembly of the State and became the nominee of the Democratic Caucus for United States Senator. As that Party was largely in the majority, his nomination was almost equivalent to an election. In Indianapolis, pending the meeting of the two Houses in joint-session, he was stricken with smallpox and died on the night of December 31, 1847, at the age of 37."

The article further stated that, while he did not excel in making his audiences think, he did excel in awakening enthusiasm: "He favored the annexation of Texas and, on the Oregon question, he stood steadfastly on the declaration of Hannegan, 'Oregon! Every foot of it or not an inch.' It was a speech he made on that question which drew from John Quincy Adams the assertion that Kennedy was the greatest natural orator the United States had ever produced."

Thus my great-grandfather Kennedy had served three terms in Congress before Lincoln arrived there in 1847, and had he not died of smallpox, he would have entered the United States Senate the same year Lincoln began his term in Congress. Parenthetically, his wife, Miriam Weaver, was a direct descendant of Clement Weaver, one of the founders of Rhode Island in 1644.

The first record of a Gallahue in a family Bible was William Gallahue, born in 1794. After reading the material, I decided to get in touch with Father, who still lived in Indianapolis, to see what else he knew about the family. He said that one of our ancestors, Captain Charles Gallahue, had served in the Revolution and raised his own company of soldiers and that Charles's brother, Jeremiah Gallahue, had been a member of the Virginia Militia. I then wrote to the War Department and received a letter stating: "The records of this office show that Charles Gallahue served in the Revolutionary War as a Captain of a Company designated Captain Charles Gallahue's Company, 11th Virginia Regiment, commanded by Colonel Daniel Morgan."

Heitman's *Historical Register of Officers of the Continental Army*, an unofficial publication, entitled to credit, shows: "Gallahue, Charles (Va.), Captain 11th Virginia—January, 1777; killed at Sag Harbor, 23rd May, 1777."

I then became interested in pursuing the matter further and consulted a local genealogist, who recommended a Mrs. Reddy of Richmond, Virginia. We began a fruitful search which ended with authenticated evidence that Jeremiah and Captain Charles Gallahue were brothers, and Jeremiah was the father of the William Gallahue of the family Bible.

Before the Revolution, Charles Gallahue served in the Prince William County Militia as captain under Colonel Henry Lee, grandfather of Robert E. Lee: "Officers of the Prince William militia in 1776 were Colonel Henry Lee, county lieutenant; William Brent, Richard Graham, and Charles Gallahue, captains; Thomas Young, sergeant major; and Dr. George Graham, surgeon." I received a photostatic copy of the commission he received direct from Congress to recruit his own company of soldiers. It was dated January 7, 1777, and signed by John Hancock, president of Congress. I also secured a list of the soldiers he recruited into his company.

By this time, I found genealogy as intriguing as a mystery story and asked Mrs. Reddy to search for the ancestors of Charles and Jeremiah Gallahue. The search led back to their parents, Darby Gallahue and his wife, whose maiden name was Charlotte Ewell and whose father, Charles Ewell, built the first capital at Williamsburg, Virginia. Charles Ewell had married Mary Ann Bertrand, whose mother was Charlotte de Jolie, daughter of Count de Jolie. John Bertrand had married Charlotte de Jolie, September 29, 1686, in St. Paul's Cathedral. Because they were Huguenots, they had fled from France to England after the Edict of Nantes. So thoroughly do the English keep their records that a friend of mine visiting London secured a photostatic copy of the marriage record of Charlotte de Jolie and John Bertrand from the files in Lambeth Palace.

Toward the end of her work, Mrs. Reddy was quite excited to find that one of the male members of my immediate family was eligible for membership in the Society of Cincinnati, one of the oldest, most exclusive societies in the United States. Its original members consisted of officers of the Continental Army who had served in the Revolution, and George Washington was its first president. Excerpts from the history of the Society:

"The Society was organized into thirteen State Societies and one of France. Louis XVI, King of France, was the Protector of the French Society. A member is elected not into the Society of Cincinnati but into the Society of the Cincinnati of one of the original thirteen states or of France.

"Succession in the Society is hereditary, that is with certain exceptions, there can be but one representative for each of the original members or from the officers of the Continental Army who were eligible in 1783 or who had died in service prior to that date.

"Many members moved West to the lands beyond the Alleghenies but their members still retained their interests in the Society—an instance of which is that a group of them named the newly founded Cincinnati after it."[7]

To become a member, I had to secure a waiver from Father and Dudley, since eligibility adheres to the eldest son. When I later became a member, I found that they examined my application and supporting evidence with the thoroughness of the F.B.I. According to the last Geographic Index of the Society, there are just six members in Indiana. Two belong to the Connecticut Society, two to the New Jersey Society, and one is from Maryland. I am the only one from Virginia.

I then turned my attention to my mother's family, and in reading the Teague manuscript, I found that Uncle Ed already had done most of the work. It was easy to complete the Teague genealogy, because they had been Quakers when they arrived in this country, and Quaker records are very complete.

Samuel Teague, Sr., was born in the vicinity of Charlotte,

South Carolina, in an unrecorded year. His son, Samuel, was born March 2, 1759, the first birth entered in the records of the meetinghouse at Bush River, South Carolina. They migrated north because of slavery, and the next son was born in Little York, Montgomery County, Ohio. The family then moved to Richmond, Indiana, where Mother was born on August 20, 1875.

The completion of the Gallahue and Teague family genealogies had a sobering effect on me. It was a turning point in my life, an awakening; I had a flash of insight that I should be doing something constructive with my personal life, since I had been so fortunate in my heritage.

Because of my great responsibility to Mother until I was thirty-seven, I became almost obsessed with the desire for personal freedom. However, I was now forty-one, and I had had this freedom for four years. I began to wonder—freedom for what? To come and go as I pleased? To have dates with a variety of girls with no entangling alliances? This kind of freedom had lost its flavor.

At this time, practically all of my dates were with Dorothy. Though I was sure I was in love with her, I was still in conflict about marriage. I had a Head and Heart dialogue with myself, which reminded me of the one Thomas Jefferson had in Paris with reference to Mrs. Maria Cosway. Jefferson wrote out his thoughts in dialogue form under the most difficult circumstances, since he had sprained his right wrist and had to write with his left hand. He had the added problem of being in love with a married woman.

After a final evening of contemplation, my comparable Head and Heart dialogue could be summed up rather simply:

Heart: You know you are deeply in love with Dorothy, and Dorothy is in love with you. Because of your life style as a bachelor, you have known literally two or three hundred girls of every sort and description. You are neither handsome nor particularly attractive to women, you just happened to be around where the action was. Sometimes love was freely given and received; at other times, the companionship was purely intellectual, or just a matter of passing enjoyment. You should know by now that it is not a question of finding a girl you will ever love more. You should ask Dorothy to marry you now and hope she accepts.

Head: What you say is true, but can you adjust yourself to a regular routine and regular hours, thus giving up your personal freedom? What is more, haven't you had your share of responsibility? Think of Dorothy; are you sure you can become a proper family man with the dual responsibilities of husband and father? No more taking off whenever and wherever you like.

Heart: Everything you say is valid, but as Pascal said, "The heart has reasons the head will never understand." I am tired of distraction and diversion that leaves an emotional vacuum. I want to put my roots down deep in marriage. If I have any spare energy or time, I want to be involved in good works such as Mental Health, to which I have given only lip service. Yes, I should gladly give up whatever is necessary in personal freedom to make marriage succeed.

I did not call Dorothy that night, but I did propose the next day, and she accepted. I found out later that, with her woman's intuition, she knew me better than I knew myself. She did not fear that I might prefer my past cut-flower life to the warmth, security, and love which should go with marriage.

I knew that it would be wise to sell my home now, for it held too many memories. Dorothy agreed, although she did not suggest it. We both thought it would be better to take an apartment until after the war, when we could acquire a home with more leisure. I sold most of the furniture and gave DePauw University some large antique pieces which my Aunt Martha had acquired in Europe. I could have stored this furniture and used it later, but it was so identified with my home that I thought Dorothy would prefer to buy everything new to suit her own taste.

Since Dorothy and I were not members of a church at this

time, we secured the services of my Unitarian minister friend, Dr. Wicks, for our marriage. We had some heart flutters both when we talked to him and when we sent out the invitations. The marriage date was set for Sunday, October 31, 1943, with a reception at the Indianapolis Athletic Club. We were doubtful about securing enough sugar for a large wedding cake, for sugar was rationed at that time. However, after much effort on Dorothy's part, she found enough ration stamps for a hundred pounds, and the chef produced a beautiful cake with spun-sugar roses and sprays of spun-sugar leaves.

We had about a hundred guests, and Uncle Ed made a special trip from California to join us. Uncle Ed was in his seventies, but he was in good health and fine spirits, and I think he had the best time of anyone after Dorothy and me. I found out later that he had long hoped Dorothy and I would get married, because he had met her before on his trips to Indianapolis and was very fond of her.

We were married on a beautiful, sunny day. In the evening, when we left the Club to drive to Louisville, it had become cloudy and much colder, and when we reached the small town of Seymour, it was sleeting heavily. Since we couldn't drive any farther, we got a room in a little hotel next to the railroad station. I had no idea how many trains ran through this town. It was the age of steam engines, and all night long the hotel seemed to shake every time a train came to a stop, squeaking its wheels and hissing steam. Any other time we probably would have complained about our accommodations, but we were happy and able to laugh the situation off.

Since I had a tremendous amount of work to do at the office, we could only plan a week's honeymoon, stopping for a few days in Louisville for the races before going on to French Lick. One of the reasons we wanted to see the races was that a friend had named a horse after me, and he was to run on the following Tuesday.

The next day dawned bright and clear, as the storm had blown itself out during the night. I had reserved a suite at the Brown Hotel in Louisville, and we arrived in time to get settled and out to the track for the first race. Dorothy also enjoyed Churchill

Downs, and we had a lovely afternoon. We were joined in the evening by my friend who owned the horse Gallahue. The next morning he invited us out to the track stables, where I was introduced to and photographed with my namesake. The horse was two years old at the time, and though not good enough for future Derby competition, he did do very well in stake races. Both owner and trainer thought he would have a good chance to win. I guess quite a few others thought so too, for they made him the favorite, and at the race the odds were down to 1.30 to 1, or almost even money on him against the field. He ran in the fourth race, and I was quite excited as the horses went to the post. I don't know whether he disapproved of my presence or what his difficulty was, but he came in fifth.

It was quite an experience to hear my name over the loudspeakers as the progress of the race was announced and a further experience, after the race, to hear people complain that that "damned Gallahue didn't even try." Next day the Louisville paper read:

> Probably the most disappointed man in the crowd yesterday was Edward Gallahue of Indianapolis. Mr. Gallahue, just married, stopped off on his honeymoon to show his bride how the horse named after him could run. But Gallahue (the horse) wasn't in a running mood yesterday and ran fifth in the fourth race after being made the $1.30 to $1 favorite.

In spite of our disappointment in Gallahue (the horse), Dorothy and I were having such a wonderful time we decided to spend the whole week in Louisville going to the races instead of going to French Lick. We went to eight races a day, or a total of forty-eight that week, and neither of us has had this sort of urge before or since.

After our honeymoon, I plunged into a rolling sea of business activities. One of my first responsibilities was a three-week series of twelve district sales meetings held throughout Indiana. In the past, I was stimulated by the meetings and enjoyed seeing all my old friends who were agents. Now that I was married, this zest was gone, and I would have preferred to stay home.

All the district meetings passed uneventfully but one. At that one, a man and a woman from the same agency drank too much, and the woman slid gently out of her meeting chair onto the floor. Some other women helped her up to a room, but this turned out to be difficult because she was as limp as a piece of liver. Her escort tried to help her, but he too needed assistance, so we stretched them out on a bed in the same room. Later on, the district manager from their territory heard about the episode and said, "My God, they aren't married!" I rushed up to the room with him, and we were relieved to find that they were sleeping peacefully, both fully clothed.

Later that evening, about two A.M., a few of us went out for some coffee before retiring. Fortunately, the street was deserted, for without any warning, one of our most distinguished and conservative officers went up to a fire plug and sprayed it well. I went over and asked him where he got this idea. He told me in an unapologetic, matter-of-fact way that all his life he had wanted to piss on a fire plug, and he couldn't think of a better time. I could not help but think how many curious inhibitions lurk in all of us.

For the next several months my life became something of a dull grind. I was up at five every morning and brought home a briefcase full of problems every night. I thought Dorothy might be about ready to crown me with a kitchen utensil, but she always had breakfast ready by six. She must have wondered, though, why we had not married sooner, when we might have had more leisure, instead of waiting until I was completely buried in business.

One venture did relieve the pressure and proved highly profitable too. In the summer of 1944, when an end to the war seemed to be in sight, I had to give thought to a complete rebuilding and reactivating of the Agents Finance Company. In 1942 we had suspended operations, because there were no new cars being made.

I had recently seen an excellent movie made by the United States Steel Company, and this furnished the germ of an idea: making a film for the Finance Company. It would be an excellent refresher course for our old agents and a source of education for the agents we expected to appoint in the near future. I took the matter up with Dudley, who thought a film too speculative and expensive a proposition, as did the directors. Ultimately, however, they gave their approval and placed complete responsibility for the project on me.

I then wrote Dick Powell to secure his opinion of Roland Reed Productions of Hollywood, producers of the United States Steel film. He replied that they were very capable and recommended them. I then wrote Roland Reed, and he sent a script writer to Indianapolis to get my ideas for the movie. I outlined a story, using a basic sales technique applicable to the sale of many products. It had five steps. For us this meant:

1. Our own agent finances cars for his clients and not only saves his insurance business but increases it, compared with the agent without the Agents Finance plan, who loses his clients' insurance to the major finance companies when the cars are financed and insured by them.

2. A conversation occurs between our agent and the agent without the plan, wherein our agent suggests that the other agent might be interested in our service too.

3. Our agent further explains the plan.

4. Our agent uses illustrations to confirm that the other agent can use our plan.

5. In the closing illustration by our agent, he takes the other agent along to a prospect and actually finances the car with the other agent present.

The script writer was agreeably surprised that I had already prepared an outline for him since this made it much easier for him to fill in the characters and story. I also helped with the technical side of the dialogue. As soon as I received the preliminary draft, Dorothy and I went to Los Angeles. There we met Roland Reed and his staff, at which time he assigned another writer to work with me on the script.

During the week we worked on the story, the owner of Gallahue (the horse) entered another horse, named after a friend of ours, at Hollywood Park. When Dorothy and I went to the track that day, we found that the horse had never won a race, and that the odds were about 25 to 1. We bet on him anyway, for sentimental reasons, and I can still visualize that race as if it were yesterday. It was a dark, murky day, and the horse broke in front, gained a lead of about four lengths, maintained this lead throughout the race, and won it. After I returned to Indianapolis, I found to my surprise that neither owner nor namesake had bet on the horse.

Another time in California, I spent a night and most of the next day on Dick Powell's ocean-going yacht. It was a beautiful boat which, prior to his ownership, had competed in races in the East, and Dick had raced it to Honolulu. It was docked in the bay at Balboa, and when we sailed it we had to stay within the bay because the war was still on. At one point, I was surprised when Dick went below and turned the helm over to me, since I had had no sailing experience except with small boats at Wawasee. There was just a light wind, which meant little maneuvering, but I found that it did not respond as quickly as smaller boats.

I never ceased to wonder how Dick had acquired all his knowledge and skills, not only in acting, directing, and producing, but in his hobbies: sailing an ocean-going boat, flying his own airplane, playing polo, and engaging in many other sports. He was an excellent example of the self-educated man.

On another occasion, we went to the Hollywood Canteen, where Marilyn Maxwell was entertaining servicemen. She did a fine job with her songs and was very popular. I have often wondered why her producers did not let her remain a brunette and go on with her singing and dancing, since she had such talent in these fields. After the show, Dorothy and I had a short visit with her.

Roland Reed and I soon started recruiting a director and cast. We were extremely fortunate to get Bill Clemens, who had directed several pictures at Warner Brothers with such stars as Boris Karloff, Bonita Granville, Mickey Rooney, Ann Sheridan, and Jane Wyman.

The principal roles were those of two insurance agents, and we were equally fortunate in getting Gene Lockhart as our agent with the plan and Stuart Erwin as the skeptical agent without the plan. The way we had the script arranged, Gene Lockhart would use the same sales points that I would have used personally, and Stu Erwin would ask every question that had actually been asked by agents. Thus the story was real, and it was educational. Any new agent would know in advance all the questions he might be asked by his clients when starting to use the plan. To Roland Reed's knowledge, neither Gene Lockhart nor Stuart Erwin had ever acted in a commercial film before, and I think the only reason they did it was to help returning servicemen who would be reentering the insurance business.

We were also particularly fortunate in our supporting cast. Mrs. Lockhart played Gene's wife; Hugh Beaumont, who later played the father in the TV series *Leave It to Beaver*, portrayed our district manager. At that time this talented young actor was preparing to enter the ministry. George Chandler, a character actor in dozens of movies, took the part of the skeptical client; and his wife was played by Dorothy Faye, who had appeared in numerous westerns. The minor parts were also played by gifted actors.

Roland Reed next prepared a budget, which was larger than I had planned, but since we also had secured better talent than I had expected, I decided to go ahead, because I felt that we ought to do the picture right or not at all. This same notion was expressed by the sales manager, who became president of one of America's largest corporations: "If you are going to promote anything major, bust them in the eye!"

I then took the final step of signing the contracts, including one to rent an RKO sound stage for one week. I had to decide whether to insure the director and cast for the week, since I realized that we would be out of business if anyone got sick or even hoarse. The premium was so high that I took a chance and went ahead without insurance.

The only thing left was to title the movie and, strangely enough, we found that we already had a good one from the advertising we had been doing. We had claimed that the Agents Finance Company was "just like having a million-dollar partner," since the local agent had this much money at his disposal to finance cars. Therefore we used the title *A Million Dollar Partner*. The resources of the company were much larger than this, but for practical purposes any agent could do a million dollars in volume if he could find the business. Before the war, agents of more than a hundred different insurance companies were using the plan, and we arranged to list these companies as a prelude to the picture.

Producing the movie was one of the most vital experiences of my life. I knew nothing about the theater or about acting, but I did know my subject and the message was in the script along with enough plot to make it interesting. Also I had had the good fortune to watch Dick Powell perform and had visited the studios a few times with guests. For some reason, I felt at home in this alien field. I think a principal reason was the informal atmosphere. After each scene, we were always visiting with someone, enjoying small talk over a Coke or coffee. There were always plenty of people around. Even for our thirty-minute movie, we had about fifty, counting cameramen, sound technicians, assistants, script girls, stage hands, et al. It was surprising to learn that a director is lucky to end up with five minutes of finished film a day; on feature pictures, even less.

Because of what I had at stake, I tried to be extremely business-like all that week. I always arrived at the studio before eight in the morning, and, on one occasion, there was a little fillip of humor. It was the day after the Presidential election in 1944, and some member of the crew got a mangy old duck from the Prop Department and hung it upside down with Dewey's name on it. Also, I occasionally took time off to watch some of the feature films being made at RKO. John Wayne and Herbert Marshall were in two separate pictures, and I always got a kick out of seeing such real pros perform.

On the last day of shooting Dorothy came out to the studio for the first time. She had stayed away because she wanted me to concentrate on the movie, and she knew how much I had at stake. We finished about two hours ahead of schedule, and since everything was already paid for, Bill Clemens, the director, suggested that Dorothy and I let the makeup men make us up, and he would direct us in our own little skit, which we could have as a memento. Dorothy was willing, but I was suddenly tired now that shooting was over. I just wanted to go somewhere and rest, and I have regretted it ever since.

On the other hand, I was sad when I said good-bye to the cast and crew, for we had built up a warm fellowship and wonderful *esprit de corps* in our week together, and I knew I would not see most of them again. I was especially grateful to Bill Clemens, who autographed the script for me: "For the best boss I ever worked for—hope it makes you a million."

The next and very important job was cutting the film and putting together what had been shot out of sequence. I can well understand the tension of making a feature picture. There is so much to be cut out and rearranged and spliced together that it is hard to tell just what you have until it is in final form. To preview a picture, the industry has a unique machine that indicates the footage as the picture is shown. It operates like a speedometer on an automobile, and in this way, if a correction has to be made, the editor knows exactly where to find it. When the movie was finally approved, we were all very pleased, and I was sure that I had something valuable. The story was so well done that I had no doubt it would give an insurance agent a good, fundamental education in financing automobiles in less than thirty minutes.

By the time we left Los Angeles, I was working on a schedule to show our movie in connection with a series of meetings. In order to get the job done thoroughly and quickly, I decided to have two series of meetings simultaneously: one in the larger cities, where we could rent one of the leading movie houses an hour or so before the regular show, then take the large group of agents to lunch; the other in the smaller towns, where we could also rent a theater or show it in smaller groups with a 16-millimeter projector, as I also had had some 16-millimeter prints made. As a follow-up to the movie, we produced a circular containing all the dialogue from the film, so the agent could always refer to it and find his answers.

After showing the film in such cities as Chicago, Cleveland, and Detroit, one of our managers said that a branch manager of the Aetna Casualty Insurance Company thought that his home office might like to see the movie. Aetna's agents were also losing business to the finance companies. Our manager also suggested showing the film to a group of insurance managers in New York. Though we did not operate in New York or Connecticut, agents of these companies did operate in the seven states we were in, so it would be effective promotion.

After we showed the picture in New York, I accepted an invitation from the Aetna Casualty Insurance Company to show it in their home office at Hartford, Connecticut. They in turn invited the leading officers from the other Hartford companies, including Travelers, Hartford, etc. The day we screened it there, I could hardly believe it; for when I made this movie, I never expected to be showing it to the leading insurance companies in the United States.

After the showing, the officers of the various companies congratulated me on the quality of the picture. This was quite a compliment, as they had all made movies themselves, although none of them, to my knowledge, had produced a movie in a major Hollywood studio with the same level of professional talent.

When the war was over, I thought that our men would be released promptly and returned to work. While this was true in some cases, in others it took months for them to get home. Then there was an adjustment period, as nearly all the men had to take refresher courses to reorient themselves. As the pressure mounted, I began feeling fatigued and did not bounce back each morning as I usually had. Therefore, in December, 1945, I decided to go to the Mayo Clinic for a checkup. I had been there several years before, accompanying Dorothy when she had a severe infection in her feet. Since her parents were divorced, only her mother was with us. In my great concern about the seriousness of Dorothy's illness I had further realized how much I cared for her.

After my examination, I was amazed when the doctor told me there was a shadow on my right lung, and he was not sure whether it was a cyst or tuberculosis. He advised me to take a guinea-pig test, in which a person swallows a tube, and from the stomach the physicians obtain a specimen which is injected into a guinea pig. If the guinea pig does not exhibit tuberculosis within six weeks, TB is eliminated from consideration. The doctor suggested I go to Arizona during this six weeks. Though I was reluctant to do so because of business conditions, I decided that I had no alternative.

To make matters worse, it was difficult for Dudley to concentrate on business, since he and Katie had recently divorced after eighteen years of married life.

Hence it was an unhappy occasion when Dorothy and I set out by car to Tucson, Arizona. Though the accommodations and climate were delightful, I could not enjoy them, for I was too apprehensive about the future.

After the six weeks were up, we decided to drive back by way of Santa Fe, New Mexico, which Dorothy had never seen. As an added interest Milton Mayer, an author friend of ours, was spending time there with some other writers. He was also one of the leaders of the Great Books Course which we attended at Butler University and we knew we would enjoy spending an evening with him on our way home.

Our hotel in Santa Fe had a casual atmosphere about it, and there was a colorful assortment of people around the lobby and dining room. Most groups tend to have a certain conformity in their dress and manner, but these people reflected individuality in their clothes, appearance, and behavior. Dorothy surmised that a number of them were artists or writers, which turned out to be true.

After lunch we got in touch with Milton Mayer, who arrived at the hotel in a sweatshirt worn inside out. When inquisitive Dorothy asked him why he was wearing his shirt this way, he said because it was dirty and he hadn't had time to have it washed. After a lively discussion about something he was writing, he invited us to a friend's home after dinner that evening. Since the friend was a Pulitzer-Prize-winning playwright, Dorothy was particularly glad to have the opportunity to meet him and his family. The author's home was in a most attractive setting. When we entered, however, we noticed that the housekeeping was not quite what we had expected. It was informal in the extreme. We were seated on a davenport opposite the coffee table, on which was a roll of toilet paper and two bottles of whiskey. As the evening wore on, I gathered that the toilet paper served for both Kleenex and cocktail napkins.

Another shock followed almost immediately. I had just given Dorothy a Russian sable scarf, which she had dropped in a chair when we entered the room. Shortly afterward, a teen-age boy sat on the scarf without noticing it. When Dorothy called it to his attention, he casually got up and hung it over another piece of furniture. He said he was sorry and hoped he had not mashed the fur on her "fox." Being a woman she was no doubt upset most by his calling her lovely sable a fox. However, after getting used to the informality of the place, we had a delightful evening, for the conversation of our host and his friends was richly colorful. When we left, Dorothy said she thought it a curious paradox that such creative, intelligent people should be such bad housekeepers.

We left the next day for Mayo Clinic via Colorado and Nebraska. The scenery was gorgeous, for it was spring, and everything seemed to be coming into bloom. Good news awaited me at the Clinic: I was advised that I did not have tuberculosis, that the spot on my lung was evidently a cyst or old scar tissue. They advised me, however, to watch the spot carefully and to have a chest X ray taken twice each year.

Shortly after our return, I became anxious to move out of our apartment and buy a house. Dorothy shared my feeling, and fortunately we found the ideal place. It was a large, Georgian-style, colonial house set on a knoll in the center of four acres of well-kept, landscaped grounds. There was a wide assortment of beautiful trees, including beeches, sugar maples, hickory, gum, and a variety of oaks. One tree that particularly caught my attention was a giant sugar maple over a hundred years old; it occupied the center of the front lawn, where it still stands like a giant sentinel.

The property was located in Williams Creek Estates, a small incorporated community adjacent to the north side of Indianapolis. The owner, who was retiring as an official of the Eli Lilly Company, had built the home only twelve years before, and he had given every consideration to quality and detail. Dorothy and I fell in love with the place and soon arranged to purchase it.

Though I never invented anything for our home, as Thomas Jefferson did for his, I am sure that I enjoyed it just as much. Dorothy and I were soon busy decorating and furnishing, and I went out once or twice a week with her to shop for various house items.

At this time, Dick Powell dropped into town for a few hours. He was flying his own plane to New York with a friend when he called me from the airport. I arranged to pick them up and drive him out to see our new home, and I invited Dick to make it his home whenever he was in Indianapolis. Unfortunately, this was the last time I saw him. He died of cancer at the peak of his career. He had furnished America with some excellent entertainment, particularly with his TV Four-Star Playhouse, and I had lost a good friend whom I greatly admired and respected.

The year 1946 was developing into the worst year in history for the automobile insurance business. During the war, automobile insurance rates had been radically lowered because of gasoline rationing, which greatly reduced the miles driven per car, and with this reduced exposure to hazards automobile accidents were correspondingly reduced. Conversely, when gasoline rationing was eliminated, the miles driven per car went up sharply, thereby causing more accidents. On the other hand, automobile insurance rates were based on an old "horse and buggy" rule of using the past year's experience instead of the current trend. Thus while all of our business on the books was written at the low rates prevailing during the war, and the present hazard was much higher, we couldn't expect a rate increase to be approved by the various insurance departments until we had the benefit of experience on our books indicating the new conditions.

As accidents continued to mount, I realized that far from making a profit, the question was how much we would lose. By nature I liked to take a progressive or offensive position, but now I was forced to settle for a defensive one. I reviewed all

our territories carefully and was forced to start eliminating large
amounts of business that had become unprofitable; but as fast
as I could plug a leak in one dam, another would rip. I felt
very much like the character in the play *Green Pastures*, who
said, "Everything that was nailed down is coming loose."

Our business problems reached a crescendo in December. The
loss ratio had buried us like a tidal wave. In addition to eliminating unprofitable business, I decided that we should also
withdraw from some outlying territories and concentrate our
business in the Midwest, with the exception of Colorado. The
Colorado account was unique, still profitable and easy to manage,
for it represented the AAA Club, and we insured only AAA
members.

As always, I discussed my plans fully with Dudley, who concurred with my proposals. Actually Dudley was letting me take
the initiative, inasmuch as he was preoccupied with personal
affairs. Following the letdown from his divorce, he had become
deeply interested in another woman and was contemplating marriage.

With great reluctance, we decided to sell our California business. We had an excellent general manager and sales manager
and more than a hundred agents. I knew, too, that California
was bound to become a great growth territory. However, our
business was growing everywhere else, in spite of our cutback, and
I felt that we had to concentrate our efforts in order to solve
our management problems. Our general manager and sales
manager in California were shocked at my decision, since not
only had they been very loyal to the company, but we were
quite close personally as well. They fully understood the reason
for my decision, and I told them that their business careers
would be protected in any sales we made; furthermore, I made
it clear that we would be delighted to have them at the home
office in Indianapolis. Both decided to stay in California, and,
fortunately, I arranged a sale that provided satisfactory employ-
ment for them. They were excellent men who later went into
business for themselves, and both have made an outstanding
success in Los Angeles. The general manager went into private

law practice, and the sales manager now has an agency of his own.

In February, 1947, when the returns were all in for the previous year, I found that we had lost 4 percent on every dollar of insurance business in effect for 1946. It might have been much worse, since our percentage of loss on auto insurance was much less than that of most companies. Also commensurate with the general chaos in the industry, the various departments had permitted some emergency rate increases to go into effect. However, we could not get the full benefits of the new rates until the old policies expired.

The tension had been taking its toll, and now that the worst of the crisis was over, I had to give some regard to my own condition. I had been extremely nervous, had not eaten or slept for months, and now I was getting irritating little tics in my arms and legs, a visible rippling of small muscles. I had been in touch with our family doctor, an outstanding internist who was aware of the strain under which I had been operating. He urged me to have a thorough physical examination, and I went to St. Vincent's Hospital, which still had the same Sister as administrator as it did when Mother was there. The Sisters could not have been more kind and understanding, giving me a large room with an extra cot in case Dorothy wished to stay overnight.

After my examination, Dr. Ritchey reported that he could not find anything organically wrong, but that I had symptoms of nervous exhaustion: the muscle jumps and a fast pulse that made me conscious of heartbeats in my ear when I laid my head on my arm to sleep. My pulse apparently did not drop below ninety even at night. It was an upsetting experience, for on the whole I had enjoyed excellent health and always seemed to be in control of myself. Now I felt like an old Model-T Ford that shook and rattled every time the motor started.

Since I felt no better after my examination, I asked Dr. Ritchey about seeing a psychiatrist friend, Dr. Mericle. He thought it would be a good idea and arranged for the psychiatrist to drop in to see me. We had been friends for a long time, and he had just recently returned from the war. He was the only psychia-

trist on the thirty-five member medical staff of Patton's 4th
Armored Division, which he joined at the Normandy landing. Like
most men just out of service, he was reluctant to talk about his
experiences, unless I asked him direct questions. Then I was so
intrigued that I often forgot my own problems. He told me of
the hard decisions he had to make about which soldiers to send
back into action, some of whom had been sent to him before.

Once, in Germany, Dr. Mericle had created a temporary
psychiatric ward in an old barn, and none other than our mutual
friend, Dr. W. C. Menninger, General in Charge of Psychiatry
for the United States Army, came by on an inspection trip.
Another time, in France, the medical staff was shaken and
nervous after a hard day of bitter fighting—the Germans had
even done some strafing behind the lines—when in walked a raw-
boned private from Tennessee. All he wanted was a prophylaxis.
The doctor stared at him in amazement and asked him where
the Hell he had been. In his hillbilly drawl, he nonchalantly explained that he had been in some cubbyhole with a French girl
he had picked up. In a burst of invective, the doctor asked him
how he could think of sex with the earth trembling from bom-
bardment and shellfire.

After several visits with me, Dr. Mericle indicated that I had
many of the symptoms the officers had just after the war. Having
been wrung dry of nervous energy in sustaining themselves from
one crisis to another, they had a king-size letdown when the war
was over. The situation is comparable to a motor running at full
throttle while the car is standing still.

When I was confined to the hospital, I would lie awake nights
wondering why I could not find an escape from my state of
anxiety. In the past, I had been ingenious enough to work my
way out of a labyrinth of problems. Now, to sustain myself I
tried to draw on all of my experience and all that I had read but
I found what many others have found, or will find: in a state of
emotional distress, intellectual introspection alone has no healing powers.

It was at this time, when the chips were down, and I was going
through an agony of suffering, that I realized for the first time
how limited my resources were. Money could only help meet

physical needs. The hundreds of books I had read and the learned talks I had heard were of no avail. Neither prestige, power, nor intellectual acuity offered sustenance. The sympathy of my friends could only help in a limited way. All that I really had that counted was the love and companionship of Dorothy and the professional knowledge and personal interest of Dr. Ritchey and Dr. Mericle. It was a dramatic example of how one-sided my life was, with all the freedom of choice when I was well, and the poverty of it when I was sick.

Six

While I was still hospitalized, I had a sudden, aching realization that I had no abiding faith to sustain me. I had already come to the end of my belief in cosmic dualism, through the following reasoning—if God had such an evil adversary of cosmic proportion, all would be chaos and the universe couldn't have been created, for God would always have been thwarted in his attempts. Also, while there were large areas of evil which I could not understand, there were also large areas representing cruelty, evil and suffering, where man was clearly responsible through the perverted use of his free will. However, as I reflected on faith in an omnipotent, compassionate, personal God, the same questions came back to haunt me. But a solution was of paramount importance to me, and it helped me to know that great men had also had this same problem, such as Goethe who stated: "The struggle between belief and unbelief is the only thing in the memoirs of humanity worth considering."

At this time a friend of mine visited me at the hospital, and I told him about my problem of not being able to get anything helpful from the various religious materials that had been passed out to me. He recommended two books to me written by Dr. Harry Emerson Fosdick, *The Modern Use of the Bible* and *A Guide to Understanding the Bible.* These books were a revelation to me, because it seemed that here was a man who anticipated all of my questions and problems. I soon found that Dr. Fosdick was a genius in his field. He was a scholar, a preacher, a teacher, a writer, and a dedicated Christian. *The Modern Use of the Bible* was composed of lectures given at Yale University when Fosdick was the Lyman Beecher Lecturer.

One of the first points mentioned by Dr. Fosdick was that "it will never do for us to play ostrich with reference to the problems which the modern use of the Bible presents . . . multitudes of people, so far from being well stabilized traditionalists, are all at sea in their religious thinking. If ever they were drilled in older uses of the Bible they have rebelled against them. Get back to the nub of their difficulty and you find it in Biblical categories which they no longer believe—miracles, demons, fiat creation, apocalyptic hopes, eternal hell, or ethical conceptions of Jehovah in the Old Testament that shock the modern conscience."[8]

Here was the substance of the very thoughts I had had, concerning a literal interpretation of the Bible. It seemed to me that my criticisms of the Bible were just as valid then as when I wrote them down for my own examination, and I saw that they were shared by Dr. Fosdick. However, he went on to show the evolution of the Bible, starting with the low level of ethics of a primitive, barbaric people, limited to a childlike conception of a primitive, barbaric, tribal God, which dramatically evolved into the ethics of the universal brotherhood, reaching a pinnacle in the person of Jesus Christ and His revelations of a personal, compassionate God.

In Dr. Fosdick's A Guide to Understanding the Bible, he uses the following examples to show the evolution of the concept of God:

Beginning with a storm god on a desert mountain, it ends with men saying, "God is a Spirit: and they that worship him must worship in spirit and truth."

Beginning with a tribal war god, leading his devotees to bloody triumph over their foes, it ends with men seeing that "God is love; and he that abideth in love abideth in God, and God abideth in him."

Beginning with a territorial deity who loved his clansmen and hated the remainder of mankind, it ends with a great multitude out of every tribe and tongue and people and nation, worshipping one universal Father.

Beginning with a god who walked in a garden in the cool of the day or who showed his back to Moses as a special favor, it ends with the God whom "no man hath seen . . . at any time" and in whom "we live, and move, and have our being."

Beginning with a god who commanded the slaughter of infants and sucklings without mercy, it ends with the God whose will it is that not "one of these little ones should perish."

Beginning with a god from whom at Sinai the people shrank in fear, saying, "Let not God speak with us, lest we die," it ends with the God to whom one prays in the solitary place and whose indwelling Spirit is our unseen friend.

Beginning with a god whose highest social vision was a tribal victory, it ends with the God whose worshipers pray for a world-wide kingdom of righteousness and peace.[9]

In his A *Guide to Understanding the Bible*, Fosdick also traces the change of character in the concept of other great ideas of the Bible: the Idea of Man, the Idea of Right and Wrong, the Idea of Suffering, the Idea of Fellowship with God, and the Idea of Immortality.

When I eliminated the literal interpretation of the Bible as the *Word of God* and accepted the point of view that it *contained* the *Word of God*, it opened up a whole new area of understanding for me. With this new viewpoint, the Bible represented the actions of a strange and different people, unfolding in a drama extending over twelve hundred years, struggling with their consciences and their concepts of God, to reach higher ground. The Jewish people were no better morally, and sometimes worse, than their contemporaries, *but they worried about it.* It also struck me as interesting that whereas the Greeks were concerned about *wisdom* and the Romans about *power*, the Jews were worried about *sin and salvation*. Here was a people, small in number, with a country insignificant compared to the leading nations of the period, Egypt, Persia, Greece, and Rome. Herodotus, the great Greek historian, writing in the fifth century B.C., doesn't even give the Jewish nation passing attention. Yet these obscure people, who chose to be obsessed with examining their consciences and searching for meaning through understanding of God, molded the course of Western civilization and the history of the world more than did the Egyptian or Persian dynasties. In some ways they achieved a more lasting influence than that of the philosophy, science, and art of the Greeks or the laws and empire-building of the Romans.

The history of the Jews contained in the Bible is a fantastically interesting phenomenon. Over the twelve hundred years covered by the Bible, their progress was anything but a steady, upward climb. They had numbers of incompetent and immoral leaders; they were always quarreling among themselves; they got lost on any number of side roads and bypasses. They even called in foreign powers to help them to eliminate their own countrymen in a civil war, were finally captured and taken into captivity, and were released only to start quarreling all over again. Any number of times, it appeared that they might be exterminated or completely absorbed by other cultures, but they seemed to have a strain in them which survived every type of adversity. Then, in the latter part of the Old Testament period, their great prophets arose with higher moral values and a higher conception of God. Finally, they reached the climax of their history, as covered in the Bible, with the birth of Jesus Christ.

With this new interpretation, the Bible came alive with great value for me. By eliminating everything that was out of character with Jesus Christ or an omnipotent, personal, compassionate God, I could dismiss a mass of irrelevant material and focus my attention on the great personalities of the Bible and share their insight, inspiration, and faith.

I now turned to Christian theology and again to the works of Dr. Fosdick and other scholars in this field. Here again, I was surprised to find that some of the leaders, and particularly Dr. Fosdick, had wrestled long and hard with some of the doctrines of Christian theology and had confronted some of the same problems which I had supposed were unique to me.

Moreover, Alfred N. Whitehead of Harvard once said: *"It would be impossible to imagine anything more unchristian than Christian theology. Christ would probably not have understood it."*

I now reached the point where I felt I should write down my own thoughts about Christian theology.

Problems of Christian Theology

1. *Virgin Birth*—I still had the same problems that I stated pre-

viously, and I could not be intellectually honest and accept the doctrine of the virgin birth of Christ.

2. *Fall of Man*—In connection with the term "fall of man," it can only mean one thing to me—he fell from a higher level. This, history and science show, is not true; man didn't fall upward out of the caves. Most anthropologists even agree that early man was a cannibal. Some theologians speak of the fall of man as "the fall of man" in terms of a shattering of a previous "innocence," but to me it simply means that he fell from the innocence of a savage, prehistoric man that had no conscience or knowledge of good and evil. Of course animals are in this category and they are certainly not "above" man. Other theologians say, "the fall and original sin" means that man's moral sense has always outrun his moral behavior-controls—and thus that he has repeatedly fallen from the securities of blissful innocence into the anxieties of the discovery that the good he would do, he doesn't do—and the evil that he now knows he shouldn't do, he does. But to me the phrase simply means that man knows he doesn't behave as well as he should. In my opinion, none of the explanations satisfactorily fit the terminology, "the fall of man."

3. *Atonement*—I cannot conceive of a God who would permit the murder of his own son in order to reconcile himself to the human race. First, if man is individually responsible for his acts, it would be the height of injustice to forgive criminals for their acts by murdering an innocent man. Second, if God wanted to forgive humanity, he didn't have to permit the best man who ever lived to be nailed to a cross in order to achieve this end. I note that even Christ asked, "My God, my God, why hast Thou forsaken me?"

Some theologians say, "In the death of Christ we see the sins of the world and of mankind made visible—this is what sin comes to!—and the love of God made effectual: love that suffers in order to reconcile the Father's rebellious children to Himself." I heartily agree with the wages of sin, but I still do not understand why Christ had to be crucified to reconcile the Father's rebellious children to Himself.

4. *Miracles*—I still had the same questions about nature miracles as I had previously, such as making the sun to stand still,

raising Lazarus from the dead, walking on water. However, I could believe the psychological and spiritual miracles of changed lives, positive changes of moral values in history, etc.

5. *Physical Resurrection of Christ*—Here again I am confronted with the same mass of conflicting reports already mentioned in my reflection on the New Testament. I have also taken into account what the Jews thought. They said that the stone was rolled away during the night and Christ's body physically removed.

When I got through examining Christian theology, I simply could not believe most of it. It seemed to me that there were a lot of stumbling blocks to the Christian faith and that man invented the theology to make it acceptable. Man had indeed been ingenious because *if* this were true, and *if* that were true, and *if, if, if*.

Dr. Fosdick had helped me greatly in understanding the Bible, as did the *Abingdon Bible Commentary*, but Christian theology only muddied the water rather than solving anything, and I felt that the Bible itself was an evolutionary development of a people struggling for a belief.

Here I was still in the agony of my search for meaning and belief, and I would have given up in despair but there was always something within me that kept me asking questions, such as those concerning the mystery of existence in general, and the existence of mind in particular. Why does the world exist? Why is the world-stuff what it is? Why do I exist?

It suddenly dawned on me that the reason that my search for God had been incredibly difficult was that I had accepted a false premise without realizing it because I felt that I had to find my belief through one of the religious systems or not at all.

I had fallen into this trap without realizing that I didn't have to accept the interpretation of God through the ideas of ages past, that I had no obligation to accept the Jewish interpretation of God or the Christian religion as modified by the Greeks, the Romans, and Western man—that the existence of God does not depend on the theology of any one religion. The theology of all religions was created from the ideas of men living in a period of scientific ignorance and superstition, and consequently their

ideas were the vintage of their time—a flat world with the earth
as the center of the universe and filled with demons, angels,
and miracles, a final judgment when people would be resur-
rected after eons of time and sent up to Heaven or down to Hell.

I now decided to try to search for meaning and belief without
going through the conduit of any religious system, and I proceeded to explore the thoughts of men who seemed to offer valid
evidence for a belief in God independent of any orthodox religion. I read the works of many, many writers, but I found that
those of five, besides Fosdick, were particularly helpful for me—
St. Augustine, William James, Elton Trueblood, Sören Kierkegaard, and Blaise Pascal. While these men were all Christians, it
seemed to me that they had arrived at a belief that was not
dependent on the Bible and Christian theology.

By now I had returned from the hospital, but my search for
meaning so possessed me that I decided to delegate my business
responsibilities, stay away from the office, and pursue my studies
at home.

I found that St. Augustine had conducted his search for meaning in much the same way that I had in my limited way. Philosophy, theology, and religion are deeply infused in his thinking,
but he went on from there and felt that data derived from reason
is only half-alive unless it is viewed in the perspective of faith
and religion, and that the converse likewise is true. As a young
man, he had been a believer in the dualistic Manichean religion: "With its very concrete tenet, expressed in a very concrete
mythology, that the universe is a battleground between two
opposing principles of Good and Evil, two co-eternal causes of
Light and Darkness, Manicheism not only had the attraction of
offering a simple answer to the problem of evil, but also one in
terms of which individual men are relieved of all the incon-
veniences of moral responsibility. It was no doubt comforting for
Saint Augustine at this time to be told that whatever evil he did
was not his own responsibility, but that of an evil principle."[10]
Since I had arrived at my own dualistic beliefs from my own
observations and reflections, my views exhibited a similarity with
the Manichaen religion, except that I thought that there were

large areas where a man exercises free will and is morally responsible for his acts.

At the conclusion of St. Augustine's search, he was consumed
with a yearning for God and reached the conclusion that "God,
Thou hast made us for Thyself and our hearts are restless until
they find their rest in Thee." Where did this yearning come
from if it wasn't real?

I now turned my attention to two works of William James,
the eminent professor of philosophy, writer, and lecturer at Harvard University, *The Varieties of Religious Experience* and *Essays
on Faith and Morals.* James helped to enlighten me in many
ways, one of which was the understanding that, even though
some of the great religious leaders have been neurotics or psycho-
paths, this fact alone did not necessarily invalidate their religious
experience.

Professor James also pointed out that the final test of the
validity of an opinion in the natural sciences and industrial arts
is invariably tested by logic and by experiment, no matter what
their author's neurosis may be, and that it should not be otherwise with religious opinion. William James also brought home
to me the validity of the will to believe in all of us. "Of some
things we feel that we are certain: we know, and we know that
we do know. There is something that gives a click inside of us,
a bell that strikes twelve, when the hands of our mental clock
have swept the dial and meet over the meridian hour."[11] We
trust the surgeon with our lives and we realize that we live our
daily lives on the basis of trust in others. Our whole financial
structure is based on trust, the will to believe being represented
by negotiable, fragile pieces of paper.

One of the high points of the will to believe is contained in
our Declaration of Independence: "We mutually pledge to each
other our lives, our fortunes and our sacred honor." And this
will to believe was vindicated by the founding fathers' actions.
Why shouldn't we give validity to our deep-rooted beliefs if
they are not contrary to reason? Again from William James: "It
is as if there were in the human consciousness a sense of reality,
a feeling of objective presence, a perception of what we may
call 'something there,' more deep and more general than any

of the special and particular 'senses' by which the current psychology supposes existent realities to be originally revealed."

I next read *The Logic of Belief* by Elton Trueblood, the Quaker philosopher and theologian, and it turned out to be the best book on the subject I have ever read. It seemed to me that Dr. Trueblood had, in effect, incorporated all the hard questions that had ever been raised through the ages in questioning belief in God. In answering these questions, he had also drawn on the answers given throughout the ages by theistic philosophers and theologians, as well as adding his own keen observations. While he knew that he could never prove or disprove God's existence in an absolute fashion and that there would be many mysteries left unsolved, such as some of the problems of evil and immorality, he did furnish the foundation for a belief in God that was intelligently acceptable.

At this point, I felt a common bond with the great Danish philosopher Sören Kierkegaard, whose: ". . . appeal is ever to the solitary, concerned individual who, not unmindful of his eternal destiny, seeks an absolute direction for his life amid the relativities of time."[12]

Why did I not profit by his experience by a leap into faith? For, as he states, ". . . only by taking the 'leap' and exercising it does one come into contact with actuality—the actuality of one's own being. The only reality accessible to any existing individual is his own ethical reality . . ."[13]

Blaise Pascal fortified my belief in the validity of innermost feelings by his insight summarized in the statement, "The heart has reasons the head will never understand."

I now decided to draw on everything I had read and thought, and to write down my thoughts somewhat in the fashion of Thomas Aquinas in the *Summa Theologica:*

LOGIC OF BELIEF WITHOUT REVELATION

DEFINITION: *The Nature of God*—When I speak of God, I am not talking about some abstraction, but about a supreme being that created the universe and everything in it. He is a personal God that knows and cares about each individual and hears our prayers.

1. PROBLEM: Either God knows everything that is going to happen and doesn't intercede, or having given man free will doesn't know Himself how man will use it.

ANSWER: I am forced to accept the second position, because if man does not have freedom he does not have responsibility, and if he does not have responsibility he does not have any moral order at all. I can only conclude that integral to God's purpose is self-limitation of even His own knowledge in order to achieve something of infinite value.

2. PROBLEM: What about sex: God's creatures have sex, but apparently God is neuter and therefore fundamentally unlike His creatures in this regard.

ANSWER: The problem here arises from the use of the word "neuter," which means something less than sexuality. A more reasonable approach is to consider something greater than sexuality. We use the word "He" as a pronoun referring to God simply as a necessary convenience, not as a reference to masculinity.

3. PROBLEM: When we speak of God as a Person, we apparently mean something quite different from what we mean when we speak of personality in men and women. God clearly does not need food, shelter, sleep, or relaxation. He has no physical pain; He never grows old; He never grows at all.

ANSWER: Personality in God is, of course, not identical with personality in man, and is not supposed to be. No thoughtful person thinks that God has a body or physical needs. All that is claimed is that God must know individuals and be concerned for them. If not, He is, in a very important sense, less than an ordinary man. What is at stake is the rejection of impersonality. Once this is rejected, we need not be deeply bothered by details which are in any case beyond our comprehension.

4. PROBLEM: The fourth problem concerns science. Science has introduced us to a very large world of incredible complexity. We get this through astronomy, on the one

hand, and through chemistry and physics, on the other.
What sort of being could observe the motion of the entire
universe, with its tremendous bodies flying in all directions
at once—and, at the same time, observe and be touched
by the actions and innermost thoughts of three billion
earthly beings, as well as those who may possibly exist on
other planets around other suns?

ANSWER: Perhaps we have the possibility of an answer in
man himself. Even man can, in a few seconds, use his
mind and imagination not only to travel through outer
space, but also backward and forward in time. Man's
computers, still in their primitive stage, can handle com-
mands in a millionth of a second, and one machine has
a memory capacity of four hundred million characters. I
don't picture God as an impersonal computer on a grand
scale, but if God is immeasurably greater than all His
creatures, including man and man-made machines, then
there should be no serious difficulty in conceiving of a
divine personality adequate to His enormous task. Indeed,
the reason for our difficulty is that of trying to limit God
to our own incapacity.

5. PROBLEM: The fifth problem is that of Divine slowness.
I am deeply perplexed by the fact that, if God has been
seeking to produce finite moral personalities He would
take so fantastically long. Also why did He follow so
many false leads on the way? Why did God create and
maintain dinosaurs for two hundred million years for no
apparent reason, while man has been here less than a million years? If we think of the whole of time on this planet
on a reduced scale as one year, man arrived only two hours
ago. Why did God postpone it?

ANSWER: The very reason for asking this question is that
we tend to limit our understanding of God to our human
perspective. If God's power is really infinite, the length
of the time is not of crucial importance. God may be
working on a time scale incomprehensible to us. If His

purpose is what we think it is, then all the eons of time are justified by the outcome, which is not yet at hand.

OBJECTION: Whatever the time scale, I don't understand how His purpose can compensate for all the agony, pain, and suffering of billions of human beings.

6. PROBLEM: The sixth problem concerns immortality. I recognize that, since a majority of human beings do not receive justice on earth, there has to be immortality in order to rectify the injustice, or God's purpose would be defeated. On the other hand, on a cosmic time scale, a human life is only the flick of an eyelash. Would this infinitesimal trial run on earth warrant continuing each life eternally, particularly monstrous lives, like Hitler's? In what form and where would the departed souls gather? It is also incredibly difficult to understand at what point in time, in his evolutionary development, man was eligible to be granted immortality. When did he change from a brute to a man? Was it in the caves, before the caves, or after the caves? It would appear that the existence of a just God hinges on immortality, and yet, it is almost impossible to conceive that each life on earth will coexist on an eternal time scale with God.

ANSWER: The basis for my belief in man's immortality will have to be a pure act of faith in God and fulfillment of His purpose.

7. PROBLEM: The seventh problem is evil. I am deeply worried about the pain and suffering in the world, much of which is plainly unjust. I am impressed by the accident of birth. How can I really believe in God's compassion when I face the fact of hunger and deformity and imbecility on the one hand, and, contrasting with these on the other hand, health of body and mind as well as unlimited economic advantages. I am also concerned about the horrible cruelty of war, whereby tens of millions of people have been injured and killed. Closer to home was my daily acquaint-

ance with pain, suffering, and death in connection with our
insurance business.

ANSWER: If the purpose of God has been that of developing moral though finite beings, it is obvious that these
beings must be given freedom. This is because forced
goodness is not genuine. If, however, persons are really
free, wrong choices will be made and these will affect the
innocent as well as the guilty, because a personal society
is inevitably one of mutual influence. This provides the
answer most often given for moral evil. Natural evil, as
represented by earthquakes and germs, is even harder to
explain, and the answer most often given is that people
often demonstrate a depth and a beauty in the face of
such calamity which we are bound to call redemptive.
Another important point is that injustice drives us straight
to a belief in the life everlasting. If God is, and if He is
just, the more we are driven to the conclusion that there is
a life to come. The only rational alternative to this conclusion is either that God's purpose has been defeated
or that there is no God.

OBJECTION: What freedom does an innocent little child
have who is born an idiot or with hopeless physical de-
formities? What freedom does a man have when he is
the victim of the various strains of bacteria and virus
that prey on the entire human race and produce a life
of suffering and death? What freedom does a man have
against the natural forces of evil, whereby he is either
maimed or killed by tornadoes, hurricanes, lightning, and
earthquakes? None of the above evils are man-made, nor
can they be charged to the perverted use of free will.
Even though some people demonstrate a depth and a
beauty in the face of calamity which we are bound to
call redemptive, others become bitter and make an avoca-
tion of henceforth making life miserable for others as
well as themselves. It is all very well for me to philosophize
about these matters, but when I see or experience them
on the cutting edge of reality, that is another matter. I

must admit that there are certain areas of evil and suffering that I simply do not understand.

CONCLUSION: An even more perplexing problem than human suffering in this world is that of goodness. What has impelled millions of people throughout history to sacrifice their health and material means and their lives for ideals for the benefit of mankind? What is the source of morality, self-sacrifice, compassion, altruism, fidelity, and hope? Where do conscience and the desire for goodness come from? Either they come from God or they are the purposeless result of the accidental assortment and behavior of atoms. If I reject the sheer accident theory, as I must, then our conscience must have come from God, and if so, His conscience must be higher than ours, since the creatures cannot rise above the Creator. And what about man's intellect? The size of the world is a great wonder, but it is much greater wonder that man has been able to measure it. Here again, man's intellect is either purely accidental or it came from God. While there are many of life's problems that are beyond my comprehension, I simply cannot accept the premise that I was created by an immoral God with no conscience, who created the universe and sent it spinning on its way with no concern for humanity. Nor can I believe that there is no God and that man has no more meaning than a stick or a stone or the paper clip on my desk. Why don't I rely on my deep-rooted feeling of will to believe and yearning? William James shared this feeling:

> Your whole subconscious life, your impulses, your faiths, your needs, your divinations, have prepared the premises, of which your consciousness now feels the weight; and something in you absolutely knows that that result must be truer than any logic-chopping rationalistic talk, however clever, that may contradict it.[14]

After meditating and reflecting on my own logic of belief, it seemed to me that I had succeeded in reducing to capsule form my problems, my answers, my objections which included the mysteries of life that remained unsolved, as well as my conclusions. At last, for the first time in my years of searching, I had an intellectually acceptable foundation for faith. The evidence seemed overwhelmingly in favor of the proposition that I had been created for a purpose, and not by sheer accident; and if I was created for a purpose, that God, my Creator, knew and cared that I existed.

Although I was not a professional scholar I felt that I had become familiar with the principal arguments presented through the ages by philosophy, psychology, and theology relative to God's existence and attributes, both negative and positive. It seemed to me that for my purpose I had finally come full circle and that there was now no question about my decision. I hadn't realized it until now but my faith had been growing by absorption—I felt a mystical relationship with God—something that words aren't yet available to define, but in my heart I knew He was there. Sometimes I had a real experience of His presence through prayer, and it was a feeling of happiness, contentment, and ecstasy I had never known before. I understand that these experiences are rare, but anyone who has ever had one will never doubt its validity, because it is as real as water to a parched throat.

However, I soon found that it was difficult for me to practice my faith in isolation. There was something terribly lonesome about it. I imagine even Jefferson and Lincoln must have had this experience of lonesomeness occasionally as a result of their refusing to join a church because they could not accept all the doctrine and dogma, even though they were both religious men of devout faith in God.

I began to wonder if there wasn't a place for me in some church. After all, I did believe in a personal God and my faith was close to Emerson Fosdick's who describes the core of his belief as follows: "For me the essence of Christianity is incarnate in the personality of Christ, and it means basic faith in God, in personality's sacredness and possibilities, and in the fundamental principles of life's conduct which Jesus of Nazareth exhibited."[15]

My first step would be to join a Christian church, and the question was, which church? I knew that it had to be a Protestant denomination because of my theology, and Dorothy and I spent months attending the services of the leading denominations. I found that the Methodist Church was now much more liberal in permitting private interpretations of the Bible and Christian theology than when I had attended Sunday school as a boy. In fact their emphasis was now on Christ, the truth contained in the New Testament, and personal experience such as John Wesley's "My heart was strangely warmed." I also found that the Quaker Church provided a wide latitude in the interpretation of the Bible and Christian theology and stressed the personal experience of the "Inner Light." I found myself attracted to these two denominations because of the theological freedom they permitted on the one hand and their emphasis on a vital, personal religious faith on the other. I was also probably influenced, at least unconsciously, by the Quaker tradition on my mother's side and the Methodist tradition on Father's side.

I talked over my opinions very thoroughly with Dorothy, who had had experience with both Methodists and Presbyterians in her family. She wanted me to make the choice because she knew how much time I had spent in studying the doctrines and theology of the various denominations. Since I was deeply impressed with both the Quaker and Methodist churches, it was difficult to make the choice. The Quaker Church seemed closer to pure religion, and the Methodist Church would afford me an opportunity to participate in a variety of good works, such as aiding private hospitals, in which they held a leadership position. It seemed to me that the Methodists were possibly overorganized since the local church had more committees than General Motors, but somehow they seemed to have enough muscle to carry this extra luggage and still retain their vitality.

I finally decided to join the Methodist Church not just as a wing of good works, but because, now that I was on solid ground with my faith, I wanted to convert the time I had spent in searching into time I could spend in doing. Specifically, I wanted to get busy as soon as possible to offer my serivces for whatever purpose to the Methodist Hospital in Indianapolis, to try to ameliorate some of the suffering I had experienced. However, before joining the Methodist Church, I had several visits with the Methodist minister discussing my theology in depth, because I wanted to be sure it was acceptable, and I didn't want to cause embarrassment to him or to myself. After our discussion, the minister invited me to join the church, because, as he said, the Methodist Church certainly had room for a person who believed in my conception of God.

Shortly afterward Dorothy and I made my decision official and became members of the Methodist Church. It was a rewarding experience—the end of one road and the beginning of another.

I shortly got in touch with Dr. Martin, the district superintendent of the Methodist Church, whom I had met previously and who was a member of the Board of Trustees of the Methodist Hospital, and asked him if there were any areas in which they needed assistance. He said indeed there were, and that they had one major problem that they had been unable to solve, the shortage of nurses. This was prior to the period of using nurses' aides or practical nurses to assist the registered nurses, since the hospital depended on students from its nursing school to do a large part of the floor duty; and it simply hadn't been able to recruit enough students to fill the classes. As a result of this situation, the hospital had forty beds unused that were desperately needed for the long list of patients waiting to be admitted. The empty beds also represented a great financial loss to the hospital. I told Dr. Martin I didn't know anything about recruiting nurses, but if he wanted me to try, to please take the matter up with the proper officials so that I would have the authority to survey the whole situation and conduct the necessary interviews to familiarize myself with the problem.

At this time I learned something about the Methodist leaders that is rather typical of them: if a person has some ability or money, or both, and wants to put it to work, the Methodists will always find something worthwhile for the person to do. Dr. Martin soon advised me that he had talked to the Executive Committee and that they would be glad to cooperate in any way possible if I would look into the critical nursing situation.

I started almost immediately gathering information, and among other things asked for a geographical distribution of the present student body. I found that the girls came from all over the state, including a large number from rural communities. This information immediately told me that whatever plan was used for recruitment would have to be on a statewide basis. After some reflection it seemed to me that the "answer" to nurse recruitment was right under our noses, through the Methodist Church. The Methodists had about 300,000 members in Indiana with a thousand churches divided into seventeen districts, supervised by superintendents, with a bishop presiding over the entire area. From an organizational standpoint, it was strikingly similar to our company setup, with district managers in charge of our various territories which I in turn supervised.

I presented a plan to Bishop Raines, who was alert to the critical nursing situation. I suggested that we hold seventeen district luncheon meetings at my expense and invite the minister and one woman representative from each church, and give them a quota of finding at least one girl interested in nursing from each church. The idea appealed to him and he gave it his approval, after talking to his cabinet, consisting of the district superintendents. We arranged for our first meeting in Indianapolis, and I personally contacted the editor of each newspaper to get the proper coverage. The shortage of nurses was such a hot subject at that time that we got excellent front-page publicity.

At this point I secured the services of one of our Systems men to assist me in setting up a comprehensive system with cards and addressograph plates for each prospect, so that we could do the proper follow-up work to the girl and through the Church. I then enlisted the help of the chaplain of the Methodist Hospital, who had a wide acquaintance throughout the state, to go with our company officer to all of the state meetings and follow the pattern of our very successful meeting in Indianapolis. The response from the Church was inspiring and the newspaper support was outstanding.

The first step in holding a meeting was to inform the press in advance and show them the newspaper articles from the previous meeting. By using this method the publicity seemed to feed on itself; after the series of meetings were held, we had a fat scrapbook full of free, well-edited publicity. The district meetings were over in a few weeks, and the results were amazing: we had over a thousand prospects for a nursing career, many of whom were old enough to apply immediately. We then followed up with a presentation at the Methodist Youth Camps, which included a movie and a talk by the head of the Nursing School, which produced several hundred more prospects.

The meetings were held in the spring and summer, and by fall, not only did the Methodist School of Nursing in Indianapolis have a full freshman class, but the Methodist schools in Fort Wayne and Gary, Indiana, did as well. In addition we now had the names of seventeen hundred more prospects for the future, all properly filed and indexed.

The results were so successful that I was asked to present the Indiana plan at the next national meeting of the Methodist hospitals held in Chicago. In response to the request of the executive head of the Methodist Hospital Association, I prepared a booklet of the step-by-step procedures of the plan and sent it to all the Methodist hospitals in the country.

At about this time my friend, Milton Mayer, the Great Books leader and writer, heard about our nurse recruitment program, and after visiting with me, stated that he thought the *Reader's Digest* might be interested in a story. He got in touch with one of the *Digest* editors he knew, and as a result he and I were invited to visit the headquarters of the *Digest* at Pleasantville, New York. There they were well aware of the generally critical nursing shortage and no one as yet had come up with an answer. We were guests at a luncheon meeting at which most of the editorial staff were present. After I explained the plan and showed the results it had produced, Milton Mayer was asked to spend some time with me and do a story. Merle Crowell, the *Reader's Digest* editor assigned to the project, asked if I would be willing to answer inquiries from responsible people and send them copies of the plan. He stated that I might make a major contribution by doing so, but cautioned me that I would probably be answering a lot of mail for a long time since they had eight million subscribers at that time and about twenty-five million total readers. I told him I would be glad to help in any way I could, so my

offer of assistance was included in the article, which appeared in
the February, 1950, issue of the *Digest*. Excerpts from the article
are as follows:

It was July, 1948. The national nurse shortage, critical for a
generation, was now desperate. The country needed something like
60,000 new nurses annually and was getting less than half that
number. Because of the shortage, there were 32,000 empty hospital
beds in the United States, and two million patients a year were
being rejected.

With its 724 beds, Indianapolis Methodist is one of the biggest
church hospitals in the world. Down to 164 student nurses, it
needed 325. Wards were closed off. Even urgent cases had to wait
days. And Methodist was better off than many hospitals.

For general manager Gallahue borrowed Dr. Claude M. McClure,
chaplain of Indianapolis Methodist Hospital; Hugh Wriggelsworth,
assistant secretary of American States Insurance Company, was
lent as his business assistant. . . .

. . . . Stories and pictures hit the front page all over the state.
"But," says Gallahue, "the publicity came out of the organizational
job. The usual mistake is to try to get the publicity first."

Results were staggering. Women's clubs, service clubs, junior
chambers of commerce, veterans' groups and sororities helped by
signing up girls or accepting recruiting responsibility at district
luncheons. In little Brazil, Indiana, storekeeper Theodore Griffith
listened to Dr. McClure and rounded up a busload of 34 Clay
County girls and brought them to Indianapolis Methodist at his
own expense. In Evansville, the non-Methodist Deaconess Hospital,
with the assistance of the Gallahue machine, enrolled the largest
entering class in its history. All three Methodist hospitals in
Indiana now have full quotas of student nurses—and a waiting list—
and 1700 bona fide prospects in the lower grades of high school are
being followed up by Ed Gallahue's agents. If your hospital, church,
club or community wants to tackle the local nursing shortage, drop
a line to Edward F. Gallahue at the American States Building,
Indianapolis 6, and ask him for the step-by-step procedure of the
"Indiana Plan." He's just a businessman, but he knows a great
deal now about nursing.[16]

The prediction of the editor, Mr. Merle Crowell, turned out to
be true. I received inquiries about the "Indiana Plan" for years
from hospitals, nursing schools, and medical associations, as well

as other interested parties. As a result I sent out over five hundred copies of the plan, which covered requests from forty-six states and several foreign countries. Obviously, the plan could be adopted by other church denominations or any group that had a widespread organization.

Milton Mayer received a praiseworthy letter from Mr. DeWitt Wallace, publisher of *Reader's Digest*, dated July 31, 1950, from which the following excerpt is taken:

> It is no news to you that your article, "How to Get Nurses Galore," was read by the largest magazine audience in the United States. But I know you will be gratified to learn that, in addition, this excellent piece was reprinted in two of our International Editions. Thus you have reached many more readers in other lands.
>
> The selection of your article for this wider distribution was a tribute to both the fundamental and the general interest of its appeal. A number of our articles are used in none of our foreign editions because their flavor and factual content are of special appeal to our United States audience.

I also received a congratulatory letter from Mr. Wallace, dated March 16, 1950, which reads as follows:

> Dear Mr. Gallahue:
>
> Merle Crowell has brought to my attention the impressive number of high grade inquiries you received as the result of the *Digest* article on the Indiana Methodist nurse recruitment program. I am deeply gratified, as I know you must be, that the piece aroused such widespread and responsible interest.
>
> I was very much impressed by the bound booklet on the plan and by your extreme thoughtfulness in sending it, with a letter of explanation, to all your inquirers. This kind of attention must have built up good will for the *Digest*, too, and we are most appreciative.
>
> Sincerely yours,
> (Signed) DeWitt Wallace

I was deeply gratified that my first venture into good works had turned out so dramatically successful.

Seven

Although I was not aware of it at the time, the experience with nurse recruitment proved to be a kind of Continental Divide in my life.

Before, in spite of some degree of success in business, the largest share of my energies had necessarily been devoted to basic conflicts—some of them within myself, some in relation to my mother and other close relatives, and some in relation to my business activities. I was not unproductive, but my productivity was within a narrow range.

Through the nursing program I suddenly awakened to the satisfactions of a different kind of concern and interest. I realized that I was emotionally free to invest my energies more objectively. The excellent publicity given to the nursing project by the *Reader's Digest* reinforced my new conviction. From that time on, I felt able to look on the investment of my energies with a freedom that had not been possible before.

This is not to say that I have experienced nothing but success since that watershed point at the age of forty-five. As the pages to follow will suggest, I subsequently encountered not only the day-to-day problems, hard decisions, ambiguities and stresses that are inevitable in any active life, but I also took on more large burdens. Yet even the largest problems have not preoccupied and confined me as the conflicts did during my first forty-five years. A potential was released, allowing me to be as constructive, as creative as my intelligence, imagination, and energy permitted. And this has been perhaps my real "success." Even my business affairs became more successful in the ordinary worldly sense precisely from the point at which I no longer remained preoccupied with them.

For some time, Dudley and I had had an understanding that when he reached age fifty, he would change his position from president to chairman of the board, and I would become president. I thus became president of the company in 1947, when I was forty-five, and I felt it was a propitious time to take stock of the past and plan for the future. In the short span of twenty-two years, our company had been through the 1929 market crash, the depression, the Second World War, and the postwar year 1946—the worst year in the history of automobile insurance.

In facing these crises, there had been no criterion to follow, no precedent, no experts to consult. Dudley and I were completely on our own. Thus by now, I had already been through more acid tests than most executives face in a lifetime. Somehow we had come out on top with a better record than the insurance industry as a whole in both our operations and investments. Consequently I felt I now had the experience to develop American States into a major company.

It seemed to me that every successful man had his own distinctive mode of action, and thus his own unique style. I had been largely dependent on my own resources since childhood, generating *within* myself my course of action. This meant, among other things, the courage to be myself, to think for myself, and to make decisions accordingly. In business, Dudley and I first dreamed of founding our own insurance company, and we saw this dream come true at an early age. However, I knew this was just the beginning, and if the company was to grow, I had to grow *ahead* of it. I had to learn to be an executive, to attract talented personnel, and to create a reservoir of knowledge of every phase of the business that I could draw upon. If I wanted success, I knew that I would have to pay the price for it, would have to direct my own course of study, seeking the requisite knowledge. Most of this was done through endless reading and long talks with experts, including an outside consultant with whom I conferred on a monthly basis.

I also knew that, if I wanted to live in a bigger world, I should acquire the rudiments of a liberal education. This nonbusiness knowledge was not only a joy in itself, but as a byproduct paid off in a practical way. It helped me to look at matters objectively, including myself. It made me realize what a relatively small orbit I operated in compared to that of the great figures of history facing the great issues of mankind. It minimized my own problems and helped me to see the forest as well as the trees.

In the specifics of management, I operated on a few precepts that worked very well for me. First, and above all, was a minimum of protocol. Advancements and awards were on a merit rather than a seniority basis. My philosophy about expenses was broad-gauged: I looked after the dollars, feeling the pennies would take care of themselves; budgets were necessary and demanded respect but not adoration. I managed to keep abreast of the specialized knowledge of the various departments, since I wanted to be capable of judging the efficiency of any department myself. This not only resulted in more efficiency but helped create a general atmosphere of empathy and understanding. I tried not to be concerned about personal recognition for myself and concentrated on making a record, taking the attitude that the recognition would take care of itself, which it usually does.

After I became president, I reviewed the entire range of company operations and emerged from my analysis with some new ideas. My first objective was to create a digest of management control by categories, whereby the information I sought would be routinely produced for me, or easily accessible. With a nerve center of significant facts, the operation would be as simple as a control panel of red, green, and yellow lights; thus I could always be alerted to important management problems. Since an insurance company of any size involves a myriad of details, represented by endless printed forms and millions of transactions, it really requires stretching one's brain to refine the material and extract the bare essentials. However, we did produce a brief outline of procedure that was so flexible it easily adapted itself to modification, regardless of the growth of the company. When we finished, we had information coming off the IBM machines monthly, including every item of income and expense from the grass roots up, starting with the agent, to the branch, to the state, to the home office department and company total. The beauty of this system was that, while formerly I looked only at the control figures, I could now easily trace any item back to its source.

We also developed a method of securing vital information by setting up a graph showing the break-even point of the loss ratio of each line of insurance, which was prepared monthly and accumulated year to date on a comparative basis with the five previous years. Hence I could not only compare our past experience, but I could tell at a glance the profit or loss on each type of insurance by looking at the percentage point above or below the break-even point on the graph. In this way I not only had our profit or loss position long before the financial statements were prepared, but I could easily locate any trouble spots.

We also included a liquidating report to test the accuracy of the claim reserves, showing the amount actually paid versus the reserve set up. This is very important to an insurance company since some personal injury claims cannot be settled for months or years, and it is vital to carry adequate reserves.

At this time I developed many timesaving devices. One was a formula for reducing reading time on outside publications, trade magazines, and investment services. Our officers already were reading all this material, each one noting the part that applied to his own department. I had a meeting with these men and arranged for them to screen the publications for me and refer to me only items of particular consequence. This system worked so well that I never missed anything of importance, and it saved me 75 percent of my reading time. I wonder how many executives are still wasting their time on a lot of extraneous material that might be readable but no more vital than yesterday's weather report.

I also began having my secretary keep a diary on my time for a sixty-day period twice a year. This was a revelation, because each time I made a review, I found that I was still doing things that someone else could do as well or better. Also I found that, by using a dozen specimen letters, my secretary could compose most of my letters without my dictating them. This saved a tremendous amount of time, yet there was no chance of error, since I always read them before signing.

I next turned my attention to sales, reviewing our entire program, and prepared a chart comparing it with our leading competitors. While we felt that we were already at an advantage on some items, we strengthened others to bring them up to par, or par plus. In addition, we introduced innovations that proved highly valuable. One was a concise record showing personal calls on our agents made by our field sales managers. Under this arrangement, we prepared a simple one-line breakdown for each agent by sales territory and recorded the date of the calls, which replaced weekly reports that soon became voluminous. (All that mattered to me was that the calls were made.) In an hour's time, I could review personally thousands of calls made by our field managers on a monthly basis and thus be assured that all of our agents were receiving proper service.

We pioneered in another sales device which no other company was using, and it proved to be most effective in securing new agents. It is customary for independent fire and casualty agents to represent several companies. In turn the companies are privileged to have several agents represent them in communities of any size. From numerous sources we secured the names of several thousand agents, and after properly screening them, we prepared a prospect list of some three thousand agents whom we decided we would like to have represent American States. We then indexed them by field sales territory and put them on our mailing list. It was the field manager's duty, whenever he was in the territory, to call personally on these agents and to turn in a report of these calls, which we recorded, thus guaranteeing to me that a certain amount of his time would be spent in cultivating new agents. This simple system was so effective in accelerating our growth that I am amazed that other companies have not adopted it, instead of depending on each field manager to improvise his own methods.

Another program that we introduced involved inviting all of our new agents to visit the home office at our expense for semi-annual meetings. This not only gave the agents an opportunity to meet the home office staff personally, but gave me a chance to evaluate our new appointees. It surprised me that most insurance companies did not follow this program; I continued to find many cases where an agent had represented a company for a number of years and had never been invited to the home office.

We also developed a device whereby we made an announcement over our intercommunications system each time an agent visited our home office. When the agent called at our reception desk, he was quite surprised and flattered to hear his name announced over the loudspeaker, as being here to see Mr. So-and-so. Very often the announcement also helped other department heads, because on occasion they also wanted to see the visiting agent about some matter pending in their department.

In addition to a survey of the company operation, I also made an evaluation of it in depth with our agents. Under this program we made arrangements with a professor at Indiana University to help us prepare a comprehensive questionnaire, asking the agent's opinion about every phase of company operations. In order to be sure that the agent would have complete freedom in expressing himself, the professor handled each questionnaire on a confidential basis. The forms were sent out by him, returned to him unsigned, and destroyed after his evaluation. The professor's report of the survey contained a wealth of information and gave us an insight into how the company looked from the agent's point of view.

On the service side of the organization, I pioneered in a new type of nationwide claim service, whereby the policyholder could get immediate action twenty-four hours a day, seven days a week. To my knowledge no company was offering this service at the time, and probably very few are doing so to this day. The weakness in claim service when the accident happened away from home, even with the national companies with branches and agents in every state, was that the service was limited to office hours—forty hours out of a 168-hour week—whereas accidents of course aren't. Under our plan, we appointed seven hundred reputable, independent attorneys and adjusters, strategically located throughout the United States beyond the territory in which we operated, who were willing to render service at any hour, providing fees were paid accordingly.

We issued a service certificate identifying the policyholder, advising him that if he had an accident beyond the radius of his agent or a local American States office, he should simply phone the home office in Indianapolis, day or night, collect. We serviced this unique arrangement quite simply by having a rotating staff of adjusters, taking these calls after office hours. These men kept a directory in their homes of the business and home phone numbers of our branch claim managers and the seven hundred independent adjusters, indexed geographically. Thus a policyholder who had an accident in a remote part of the United States, even at two in the morning, could call our home office direct, and our telephone operator would transfer the call to our claim manager at his home. After the policyholder identified himself, the manager would then either give him the necessary instructions or, in the case of a serious accident with personal injuries, call one of our adjusters, who then proceeded immediately to the scene of the accident. The adjuster was told to handle the claim on an emergency basis until the policyholder's coverage was verified the next day.

We received many testimonial letters from our policyholders, wondering how we managed to have adjusters personally reach them within an hour or two after an accident, even in an isolated part of the country and in the wee hours of the morning. The deepest gratitude was expressed when the accident involved personal injuries, and we furnished the best in medical or hospital care in parts of the country where the policyholders were total strangers.

After completing my survey of the company's operation, I turned to organizing our staff. I found that we had twelve key officers responsible for all aspects of the business. I organized this group officially into the Administrative Committee, which met on a monthly basis. I attended the first meeting but advised that I would only meet with them occasionally, unless something special developed. I wanted this committee to be a challenge to them to develop their own ideas. I arranged for the senior officers to rotate the chairmanship and to keep minutes of all meetings, which would show that each of the twelve officers was called upon for comments at each meeting. I further stated that this was their opportunity to present creative ideas, and if they had any suggestions about how the company could operate to better advantage, they should feel free to say so and put it in the record. The monthly review of minutes was an excellent device by which I could judge the creative ideas of our staff, as well as their maturity in making decisions.

This committee was so effective that it was the only one I ever appointed to report to me. There were numerous subcommittees, but this information was funneled through members of the Administrative Committee. The company had only one other major committee, a Finance Committee which reported to the Board of Directors.

I doubt if there was, or is, an insurance company of our size in the country that does not have a number of major committees eating away the valuable time of their key men. My feeling is that, knowingly or unknowingly, many committees are formed merely as a protective device for sharing responsibility. To me, unnecessary committees are the greatest handicap to dynamic, progressive leadership. If a person has ability and confidence in himself, he ought to have the courage of his convictions. The other side of the coin of authority is responsibility. As president of the company, I was the chief executive officer, and whatever faults I had, they did not include reluctance to assume responsibility. In fact I preferred it this way; there was no buck-passing, and I was willing to take credit or blame for my actions. I think my attitude served as a good example to the key men, who were encouraged thereby to seek authority and responsibility. The result was that we developed strong leadership.

I discovered another key element to being a competent executive. The movie version of a top executive is that of a man who delegates responsibility and then forgets about it, but any competent executive knows that this is not a fully realistic portrait. The secret is not simply to delegate responsibility, but to set up a "suspense" file to be sure that the officer reports back that the mission was accomplished as planned, or shows good reasons why it wasn't. This gives the executive the dual advantage of not doing anything that someone else can do as well or better, and of being sure that the task is being carried to completion by competent hands.

I also initiated other programs which added security and the warmth of human understanding to our firm. We introduced a liberal retirement program and adopted a policy on hardship cases that was almost extravagant. We could not write any rules on the subject, but we developed a tradition of taking care of our own. For example, one of our officers who had just reported to the company was involved in an automobile accident resulting in injuries so serious that he could not assume his position for a year. However, we paid his full salary during this period. We had several other critical cases that we handled in the same way, in addition to numerous situations of a less serious nature. This demonstrated that we were not just operating an impersonal, efficient machine, but rather a company with a heart.

We now had the personnel and a management team second to none for a company our size, and the force of our dynamic leadership soon made itself felt. Within a short time, we began to ride the crest of a wave of growth and prosperity that culminated in 1954 with the American States declaring a stock split and dividend amounting to fifteen shares of new common stock for each share previously held. It was a bonanza for the stockholders, and the personnel were liberally rewarded with increased incomes.

Besides my increased business activities, I soon was engaged in a number of good works. Following my success with nurse recruitment and the attendant publicity from the *Reader's Digest* and numerous newspaper articles, I was asked to take part in a number of other activities. I was invited to become a member of the Board of the Methodist Hospital, and I accepted this invitation with enthusiasm, since I knew there would be plenty to do there to ameliorate suffering.

Also my friend Dr. Mericle introduced me to another psychiatrist who was interested in activating the Indiana Mental Health Association. This organization had existed on paper for a number of years, but had never gotten off the ground, though a few members met periodically. The first meeting I attended was held in the basement of a Unitarian church with about a dozen people present. After discussing the need for a strong mental health organization in the state, we heard the treasurer's report: to my amazement, there was only $186 in the bank.

I was further shocked by reports of the chaotic conditions existing in our state mental hospitals; moreover, there was as little organization as money to do anything about them. I did not need anyone to spur me on in this field, for I knew from my own experience with Mother how tragic mental illness is, even when one receives the best in psychiatric care. And the patients in our state institutions did not have a chance to secure help worthy of the name.

I was appointed to a small committee assigned to breathe new life into the organization. We organized a nonprofit corporation with eighteen board members, six of whom were psychiatrists, to assure proper leadership and professional standing. I wound up as president of the newly organized Indiana Mental Health Association, and then my problems began.

After talking to the local psychiatrists, I got in touch with Drs. Karl and William Menninger for advice on establishing and financing a statewide organization. I had kept in touch with them off and on since Mother had been there, and they were very helpful in giving me sound advice. They agreed that the first thing we needed was an executive director, trained in the mental health field, together with an office and secretary. They recommended a man they knew, Walter Argow. After talking with the Drs. Menninger, I went out with great enthusiasm to raise the money and get the show on the road.

The first year's budget amounted to a modest $20,000 and I expected no difficulty in raising it. Much to my dismay and disillusionment, I could not find anyone sufficiently interested in mental health to back our organization financially. The other volunteers had the same lack of success, and after a couple of months' work, we had less than $5,000 to show for our efforts. Since I was almost a fanatic about getting started, I decided to finance the program myself the first year. As I recall, I made a gift of $15,000 which, with the few thousand we had raised, was sufficient to open and equip an office and to employ a director and secretary. We were successful in securing the services of

Walter Argow as executive director and immediately began a series of meetings with our directors and volunteers to get the organization rolling.

It was my goal to organize county societies and eventually to have one chapter in each county. As my first experience in working with a volunteer organization in the embryo stage, it was a novel adventure. The organization was the ultimate in representing a mixed group, ranging from highly trained psychiatrists to well-meaning folk who were completely inept and inexperienced in making decisions at the policy level. In some cases, the volunteers were using their time with us as an outlet to work off some of their own emotional problems.

However, as time went on, several able people joined our cause, and it was possible to begin to build a strong team with leadership in the right places. Though I had to contribute a sizable part of the budget the second year too, we were beginning to get support from influential sources, and several new chapters organized throughout the state.

One of my most disturbing experiences came with a visit to the state mental hospital at Madison, Indiana. From the outside, it appeared to be an ideal facility. The hospital was located on a bluff with a beautiful view of the Ohio River. There were attractive buildings surrounded by spacious grounds. On the inside, it was clean enough, but everything was bare and drab; and as Walter Argow and I inspected it, we felt that a melancholy wretchedness permeated the atmosphere. We did not encounter the groans, weeping, and outcries of people suffering acute physical pain, but rather the agony of twisted, tortured, damned souls, reflected in their faces, their posture, and their movements. It reminded me of Mark Twain's "poor, damned human race." These patients were the victims of outrageous misfortune with no psychiatric program to help them.

I had been deeply motivated to help before this experience, but now I felt pushed to the brink of irrationality. For days I was so depressed that I finally had a long visit with a psychiatrist on our Board. He said, "Ed, you are acting as if you are personally responsible for the fate of these unfortunate people. You have

an obligation to help them as a member of society, but you are
not responsible for their illness. Don't play God with yourself.
As president of the Mental Health Association, you can't take
14,000 patients to bed with you every night and do anything
effective yourself." It was a difficult lesson for me to learn, since I
am inclined to identify too closely with the sufferer and say,
"There but for the grace of God go I." A dose of identity with
suffering is good—it gives you compassion and empathy; but an
overdose is bad—you dare not drown yourself in it.

I asked the psychiatrist about my motivation. Was the reason
for it guilt, was it Kant's "categorical imperative," or was it a
spiritual inspiration? He said he did not know, and it would take
a lot of time to throw any light on it. However, he added that he
did not think the reason for my motivation should be of paramount importance to me, as it certainly was not to the people
who needed assistance. He felt that the important thing was to
dedicate myself to improving facilities for the mentally ill, and
if they received this help, he was sure that the patient and the
bereaved family would not be concerned with my motivation. I
soon realized that from a practical standpoint motivation made
no difference to anyone, provided I got the job done.

At about this time, Walter Argow accepted an offer from another mental health organization, where most of his time would
be spent in the field of teaching and education, which he preferred to organization and fund raising. Fortunately, his succes-
sor, Joe Brown, offered just what our problems demanded. He
handled the position like a capable business executive with a wide
variety of talents. With his versatile dynamic personality, he attracted top leadership throughout the state.

As we developed interest in chapters throughout Indiana, we
also started an effective educational program with our legislators.
I knew from my experience with the insurance lobby that one
dare not wait until the legislature is in session to start an educational program. This especially had to be avoided in Indiana,
where the legislature only meets for sixty days every two years
during which members are buried with bills and pressure. We
found that, by approaching the legislators between sessions, most

were willing to listen, since we obviously were not selfishly motivated. In addition to visiting with the legislators, we approached the nominees of both parties at election time to solicit their support too.

By this time, I had another advantage which was very helpful to our cause. Dr. William Menninger had invited me to become a member of the Board of Governors of the Menninger Foundation. I was delighted to accept this membership since Menninger's was not only providing excellent care for patients, but was leading the world in the number of psychiatrists being educated. In addition, it was firmly on the frontier of new knowledge with its wide variety of research and educational programs.

Now that I had a close relationship with him, I asked Dr. William Menninger to address both houses of our legislature just after the opening session. The excellent attendance included practically all the representatives and senators as well as the governor and lieutenant governor. His address achieved fine results, because he was not only able to awaken the legislators' consciences, but did much to remove the stigma of mental illness by demonstrating that there should be no more shame connected with it than with appendicitis. It was, he said, only ignorance of the facts that caused people to take a dim view of mental illness, and these facts took on a different light when put in proper focus under the spotlight of medical science. Dr. Menninger also pointed out that, from a purely economic standpoint, it is cheaper for a state to spend millions on effective psychiatric treatment to cure the patients and return them to society than to continue to spend tens of millions for more buildings, in which they get only custodial care.

I served two terms as president of the Indiana Mental Health Association and received an unexpected citation at the end of my second term in 1950. And though I have always retained my interest, another project came along that took most of my available time for the next several years. I felt that I had made some contribution in getting the new association off the ground, and it was gratifying to observe the phenomenal progress made under the executive director, Joe Brown, and the outstanding leadership that came to the front for mental health in our state.

We also received assistance from the National Association, as the newspapers duly noted:

HOOSIER MENTAL HEALTH PROGRAM
LAUDED AS OUTSTANDING IN U.S.

Indiana's mental health program was lauded as the most outstanding in the United States here last night by Mrs. A. Felix Du Pont, Sr. of Wilmington, Del., an official of the National Association for Mental Health.

Mrs. Du Pont addressed nearly 500 persons at a dinner in the Claypool Hotel kicking off a state fund drive for $300,000 to aid the mentally ill.

Highlights of the Indiana program included the new 250-bed, 7-million-dollar LaRue Carter Hospital, offering short-term intensive care for screening and evaluation before patients were assigned to another institution; and a new 2,000-bed, 20-million-dollar hospital for long-term care. The state expenditure for mental health care in 1945 was 4½ million dollars compared with 55½ million dollars in 1968 with only a 12 percent increase of patients. The Indiana Mental Health Association now has chapters in each county, with a membership of over 30,000 compared to a handful when I attended the first meeting. In 1968 the Association raised $666,000 for its budget compared to $20,000 in 1949 and $186 in the bank when I became president.

Another important development was the Gold Ladies organization made up of women who do volunteer work in all the mental hospitals. Among other things, they see that each of the fourteen thousand patients receives a Christmas present and takes part in holiday activities. No longer do the mental patients of Indiana represent the forgotten man, relegated to the scrap heap of society. The Mental Health Association is alert at all times to their problems, supported by enlightened government officials and the accelerated awakening of the public.

It was at this time that I had a new and deeply felt insight—a potent awareness that the greatest healing power for one's own suffering is helping to alleviate the suffering of others.

After I had been on the Methodist Hospital Board about one year, the nursing school classes had a full quota of students, which was adequate for operating the hospital at capacity. However, it soon became apparent that, even though the Indianapolis hospitals were using their full facilities, there was a critical shortage of hospital beds in the area. All informed people, such as members of the Medical Society, the Chamber of Commerce, and industrial leaders were aware of this problem, but no one had come up with a satisfactory solution, since there was no uniformity of opinion.

After reflection on this problem, I felt that we should have a survey made by outside experts who could give us a documented, objective opinion. I made an investigation through several sources and found that there were at least two firms competent to handle the survey, and that the cost would be a modest $25,000. In order to bring the idea into being, I put up the first $5,000 and solicited gifts from two hospitals with which I was connected, the Methodist Hospital and a small private psychiatric hospital of which I was then president. I then secured the approval of a gift from the Indianapolis Medical Society, the Chamber of Commerce, and the Lilly Endowment. The Indianapolis Foundation also supported the survey, and the president suggested that we form a nonprofit corporation to receive the money and be responsible for the survey. I then called on the senior partner of one of our leading law firms, who generously agreed to contribute legal services. We incorporated the Indianapolis Hospital Development Association with a board of seven directors, and at the first meeting I found myself president of the new organization. The year was 1950, and I was forty-eight.

When the survey was completed, its results put forth the astounding proposal that we conduct a hospital campaign for 12 million dollars to build a new Community Hospital and to enlarge the facilities of the other hospitals. My reason for calling 12 million dollars an astounding figure is that, to my knowledge, Indianapolis had never raised over two million voluntary dollars, which was the budget of the Community Fund at that time.

At this point, I knew we should have to strengthen and broaden our leadership if we were to have a successful fund drive. Most of my business contacts were in the financial world, and we needed a man of wide acquaintance with the entire business community. I felt that, in addition to my position as president, we needed a chairman of the board, and I knew just the right man. George Kuhn had long been active in civic affairs, having been president of the Chamber of Commerce and the Community Fund and associated with many other good causes. He was particularly interested in the critical shortage of hospital beds. I asked him to be chairman of the board and, fortunately, he accepted. We started immediately by enlarging our board to include more members of the medical profession, additional civic and industrial leaders, and leading representatives of labor and the various religious faiths.

We next set up a few important committees and began interviewing fund-raising firms. At this time, we decided that whatever we did we wanted to do without the help of any federal funds. This was a further indication that Indianapolis was one of the last outposts of rugged individualism and independence, which it always has reflected politically.

After our full board was properly organized and ready to select the fund-raising firm, George and I agreed to rotate our positions as chairman and president in order to get some of our top people more deeply involved. We called on six community leaders who we thought could do an outstanding job in our positions, but to our surprise and disappointment we found no takers. In every interview, we sensed an undercurrent of skepticism about the ability of Indianapolis to mount a 12-million-dollar hospital campaign. Since we did not want to cheapen our positions by shopping for successors indefinitely, we decided to continue in the positions of chairman and president ourselves.

By now, I was completely dedicated to improving our hospital situation and so was George. I can well remember his remark when we decided to go ahead ourselves: "Ed, I will stay with you if we end up playing pinochle together."

The Board of the Indianapolis Hospital Development Association eventually voted to conduct a campaign and try to raise 12 million dollars in private funds. We then secured the services of a professional firm to help us and proceeded to set up the campaign organization. We were successful in getting an excellent campaign chairman and the right leaders for the major divisions.

Still, under the best of circumstances, it is incredibly difficult
to build a complete fund-raising organization of volunteers from
scratch. The leaders have to be either extremely dedicated or a
little "off their rocker" or both; several of us were both, and it
seemed that we did nothing but go to meetings, plan the work,
and work the plan. I know that it took most of my own time
for over a year, during which I was away from my office more
than I was in it.

There were endless frustrations. The volunteers in some divisions failed to follow through with their assignments. In business,
one can operate with precision through trained personnel, but
with volunteers one can only hope for the best. Many times, at
the end of the day, I felt at one with Voltaire when he remarked:

> My brain at morn with wisest projects teems
> While folly chases folly all the day.[17]

However, the top leaders were magnificent.

I was particularly thrilled by the two largest gifts: the Eli
Lilly Company and the Lilly Endowment made a combined
gift of $1,200,000 or 10 percent of the total goal, and General
Motors gave one million dollars. The pledge card for the gift
from Lilly's was given to me personally by one of the senior
officers in recognition of my pioneer work. I have a photograph
of this occasion in my office, and I have looked at it more than
once when I have become discouraged in subsequent fund-raising
ventures.

Much to the gratification of our leaders and thousands of
volunteers, we completed the Hospital Campaign on time, December, 1953, and surpassed our goal by raising $12,500,000. As the
money was paid in, it was invested immediately, and since it
took several years to complete the hospital construction, the
interest on our investments more than paid for the total cost of
the campaign so that everyone knew that 100 cents of every
dollar of his gift went into hospital construction. In addition,
after all commitments were made, there was still sufficient cash
to keep a skeleton staff together and some seed money left for
start-up expenses for a later campaign. At this point, I could not

help reflecting on how lucky I had been with an idea and $25,000.

We received excellent editorials from our Indianapolis newspapers, one called "Our Finest Hour," another, "Indianapolis Shows the Nation." And the campaign attracted national attention, not so much because of the amount of money raised as because it came from private funds with no request for federal assistance. One article appeared in the *Saturday Evening Post* and *Reader's Digest* called "They Don't Want Uncle's Money." And President Eisenhower sent congratulations to our campaign chairman, Willis B. Conner, Jr.:

> This success is evidence, furthermore, of a most commendable spirit of self-reliance in your community. Accomplished without the participation of federal or local government, this campaign is a stirring example to all citizens, everywhere, who are striving for the improvement of their respective communities.

One precampaign development had to do with the site for the new 5-million-dollar Community Hospital, which was to be located in Irvington, where I had grown up. George Kuhn and I found an ideal location of twenty-eight acres, which was then on the verge of being sold to settle an estate. Since there was no money available at that time, and George and I were so sold on the location, we bought the ground ourselves. Later I made a gift to the campaign of this site as a memorial to my mother. The plaque reads:

> The Twenty-Eight Acre Site on Which This Hospital Is Built
> Was Given by Edward F. Gallahue
> in Memory Of His Mother Pearle Marie Gallahue.

I was extremely gratified to have the financial capacity to do this for several reasons. First of all, it was an appropriate and living memorial to Mother; secondly, I had a sentimental interest in Irvington; and last, it was located less than a quarter mile north of the old Irvington golf course where I caddied as a boy. When the ground-breaking ceremonies were held, Vice-President Nixon was on the scene with complimentary remarks about the citizens of Indianapolis and I was presented with an engraved silver cup.

Although Dorothy and I went to occasional parties and kept in touch with our friends, we spent most of our spare time at home, pursuing our various interests. I was now enjoying a measure of contentment and happiness I had never known, and Dorothy assured me that she shared this feeling. I had my share of problems during the day, but now I had a delightful environment to which to return at day's end. The only thing I missed was vigorous health. I was in generally good condition organically, but I noticed that I couldn't endure pressure as before. I became tired sooner and developed a nervous colon, which acted as a barometer of pressure. In addition, following an emergency operation for appendicitis, I was left with some troublesome adhesions.

The one very sad personal experience I had during this period was that Uncle Ed died in an automobile accident in 1948, at age eighty-one, when he was driving home one afternoon. My cousin Jack told me that he had been taking naps in the afternoon, and evidently he became sleepy while driving that particular day. I had great affection for him, and he seemed almost immortal to me, for even in his eighties he had continued all his activities, playing golf, driving a car, and going about his jaunty life as usual.

He was brought back to Richmond, Indiana, for burial in the family lot in the cemetery that lies in the shadow of Earlham College, which he had attended. It was this same cemetery that he and his friends had sometimes walked through with their dates when he was in college. The cemetery provided more privacy than the campus. If there was any way to soften the blow of the burial of a loved one, it was accomplished this day. There was something serenely beautiful about the place, with its rolling ground and lovely forest trees, and the minister conducted the service with the quiet reassurance that is traditional in the deep faith of the Quakers.

A short time later my stepmother also died after a long illness. She adored Father to the end, and he, in turn, was with her constantly, showing more sympathy and attention than I had ever seen before. However, after my stepmother died, Father developed the habit of phoning me every evening when I was in town. I know it made him feel important to discuss business with me, but this added extra strain when I was already over-taxed. At other times, he would write me about the great achievements of the New Deal, being an ardent Democrat and great admirer of Franklin D. Roosevelt. He had written F.D.R. often when he was President, and the letters he received were always on White House stationery and occasionally bore Roosevelt's signature. Father's letters on this subject were very trying, since I was a Republican and knew he killed my vote every time I went to the polls.

Father would also send me grandiose plans detailing what some of our large corporations should do about developing new products, mergers, etc. Strangely enough, one of his ideas is now a fact: the merger of the Pennsylvania and New York Central Railroads. If he had had the ability to analyze as well as to dream, he no doubt would have been a success. Unfortunately, his life was like a river that rushed headlong down a mountainside with terrific energy, but with no provision for harnessing its powers. It was tragic that a man with such a luxury of ideas, health, and energy could not organize himself and direct his ability into constructive channels. In his business life, he made the same mistake over and over again—the foolish extension of credit to make a dramatic sales record. Of course, this was only a symptom of a deeper emotional problem—his irrational hunger for acclaim and recognition. And when he couldn't achieve it, he resorted to the synthetic world of alcohol.

Throughout life, I have met similar personalities varying only in degree. I have also known many more men who could organize themselves for a job, but who had no creative ability. By contrast, if a man has creative ideas plus the energy and personality to translate them into action, he has an almost foolproof foundation for success. This kind of man can dream his dreams and see at least some of them fulfilled: the creative thinker and the man of action, the scholar and the salesman, a man with a compass in his head and a magnet in his pocket—these blends are rare, and they are usually awarded a high degree of achievement.

On the other side of the coin of family affairs, Dudley got married again. This time he had a quiet wedding in his home in Brown County. He married a very attractive girl, and it was my deepest wish that he would find happiness in his new marriage.

In 1951 we had some unusual excitement in our own home. Dorothy was pregnant! We had wanted a child for a long time and had both been told by our doctors that there was no reason why we should not have children. It was evidently just one of those situations that took nature a while to get around to. Since I was now forty-nine and Dorothy was thirty-seven, we approached the obstetrician with some apprehension. However, he reassured us and gave Dorothy a program to follow between trips to his office. Although it was the longest nine months of our lives, things went along well until she went into labor, whereupon she had a very difficult time for three days. I was in and out of the hospital and spent the third night there myself. When the baby was finally born at 4:00 A.M. on September 23, 1951, we were both completely exhausted, though my worry was nothing compared to her ordeal.

I was somewhat amazed when I saw my baby daughter. I didn't realize newborn infants were so small, and since she, as well as her mother, had had a hard time, she was blue around the mouth. Even her little fingers were blue. I was greatly concerned, but the obstetrician assured me that she would be all right although the birth had been a very difficult one. We had around-the-clock private-duty nurses and I insisted that we take them home with us to look after Dorothy and our daughter, whom we named Gloria Ann.

The pediatrician, who was a good friend, was now in charge, and I am sure that he must have been amused at my behavior and the behavior of the special nurses. They took over our house as if they owned the place. Besides the room and bath for Gloria, they used a guest room and bath; then they invaded my private bathroom with various baby gadgets, because it was larger. I explained my situation to Dr. Rust and asked him if he had any idea what the hell was going on around my house. He said, "Ed, I realize why you are disturbed, but at a time like this, fathers aren't really good for anything except to pay the bills."

He further warned me that little babies aren't interested in anything but themselves and their mothers. He said, "I don't want to take the romance out of your new fatherhood, but your daughter won't pay much attention to you for a year or two. Furthermore, while I love children and have three daughters of my own, for the first year or two, babies are just selfish, smelly little animals." I found this to be absolutely true as far as I was concerned, and it was quite an adjustment to make, as now everything around the home had to be attuned to the care of Gloria. Our home, once quiet, orderly, and peaceful, was now in an uproar.

I ran into a psychiatrist friend who asked me how I was getting along with the baby. I told him about my problems, and he smiled and said, "I wouldn't worry about it, Ed, if I were you. Any man who is *boss* in his own home is a mean son of a bitch." I didn't doubt for a moment that my troubles were all worth it, and I knew I could love my daughter if I had a chance, but I could not help being stunned at my misconceptions concerning marriage and childhood.

I had been greatly concerned about my ability to give up my personal freedom and adjust to marriage, but this had turned out to be a mirage, since I had no desire to return to my old way of life. Besides my love for Dorothy, I mused that maybe it was easier to be virtuous as you got older. It reminded me of a little verse about David and Solomon:

> King David and King Solomon
> Lived merry, merry lives,
> With many, many concubines,
> And many, many wives.
>
> But when they both were older
> And tired and full of qualms,
> King Solomon wrote the Proverbs
> And King David wrote the Psalms.[18]

I didn't write any psalms, but I spent long hours thinking up a name for our home that would be appropriate to Gloria, and I finally came up with Gloriana. It not only fit her name, Gloria and Ann, but neatly included the last syllable of our state.

Eight

A few months after Dr. Will Menninger appeared before the Indiana legislature in behalf of the mental health campaign, I arranged a luncheon for him with about one hundred leading businessmen, so that he could tell them about the Menninger Foundation. I had already secured some gifts for the Foundation, and I felt that many more responsible people would become interested if only they knew about the great medical program in Topeka. He and his wife stayed at our home overnight as they always did when they were in the city. Dorothy and I looked forward to these occasions, since being with them was always stimulating and educational.

During the evening, I brought up one of my favorite subjects, the alliance of psychiatry and religion. I said it seemed that psychiatry had to do with the behavior of man during his life span, but had nothing to say about the purpose of life and the ultimate destiny of man. It is difficult to analyze an emotionally disturbed person, but even if the diagnosis is correct, the patient often needs a new set of values, which is available only through religion.

At the time of Job's affliction, his insight was prophetic:

> What is my strength, that I should hope
> And what is mine end, that I should prolong my life?

This double question is echoed countless times today by troubled people.

One might say, in an age of specialization, that the first query belongs to the realm of the psychiatrist: what is the individual's strength, his personality assets for enduring the stresses of life?

The second asks about the meaning and destiny of life and therefore is referred to the clergy.

Distressed people, however, are not likely to pause in the depths of their misery to work out this neat distinction. They want help "all over." I suggested that the Menninger Foundation sponsor a high-level conference of psychiatrists and theologians which I would finance. Will Menninger felt that this was an excellent idea, promised to discuss it with his brother, Dr. Karl Menninger, and report back to me. Karl Menninger liked the idea very much and agreed to serve as chairman of the conference.

The conference was held at the Menninger Foundation, Topeka, Kansas, on May 13 and 14, 1954. The Foundation did me the honor of calling it the "Gallahue Conference on Psychiatry and Religion." Dr. Karl Menninger had wisely kept the number of participants down to thirty to encourage open and intimate discussion. Roughly half were from the Menninger community, the other half from outside. Similarly, about half were psychiatrists, and about half were theologians representing the three major faiths. We met for two days of intensive discussion, and included an evening meeting for the entire Menninger community. In his opening statement to the conference, Dr. Karl Menninger said that its aim, as he saw it, was for the representatives of religion and of psychiatry to evolve a plan of cooperation.

The first conference reconnoitered the overall relationship between religion and psychiatry. To what extent did they have common goals? To what extent were they attached to radically different understandings of life's meaning and purpose? Did a psychiatrist have to be atheistic or agnostic, and must a religionist be dogmatic? Both religion and psychiatry have divided into multiple sects, each with its own doctrines, its own saints and apostolic successions, and its own propagandist. To what extent are both "healers," and in what degree are they interpreters of life's meaning? Practically speaking, can they work together, or is this expecting the impossible?

Dr. Frederick J. Hacker, head of the Hacker Clinic and the Hacker Foundation, Beverly Hills, California, stated that at least the climate was favorable for such a discussion: "Gone are the days when science, sure of its inevitable progress, looked at religion with the certainty of enlightened reason, relegating religious manifestations to the role of a developmental phase of collective immaturity which would slowly or abruptly disappear under the impact of more complete scientific knowledge. On the other side, religion, deploring the rationalistic error of a materialistic world view, considered itself the sole preserver and guardian of the spiritual that had to be defended against godless positivism."

It was, needless to say, an additional advantage to have Dr. Karl Menninger chair the conference. I never saw his genius so well demonstrated as in his capacity to foster true dialogue at that first meeting. Before the conference closed, Dr. Karl asked, "Should we have another?" The response was unanimously favorable.

The participants proposed that each subsequent conference have a basic theme of general interest to both psychiatrists and theologians. For the next conference, the subject of freedom was selected. It also was agreed that preparatory papers, which every participant could read in advance, be submitted before each conference.

The next conference was held on May 23 and 24, 1955, just one year after the first. Virtually all the participants had made available introductory statements in advance, and these had been duplicated and sent to others, including me. Consequently, I had been thinking seriously about "freedom" even before the conference convened. Most of the participants had been with us the year before. But there were a few new and invariably brilliant faces. We had thirty-two conferees.

If there is a more deceptively simple subject than human freedom, or free will, I have never found it. Many of the problem areas were clearly indicated in the advance papers, so that I had some preparation when the dialogue began. But the discussions went far beyond the advance papers. I kept thinking, "This is an *explosion* of knowledge." I could never predict where the next point would come from. A theologian might present a defense of science, or a psychiatrist might tell the clergy to be less worldly. The brilliance and versatility of our group was astounding.

Even more than the previous year, I was impressed with the growing mutual respect of the participants. I saw more clearly than ever that even the truly great psychiatrists and the theologians in our group had, before the meeting, tended to see one another in stereotyped terms. In the actual encounter stereotypes broke down. Nobody could be neatly pigeonholed. This applied not only to psychiatrists and theologians, but to different brands of psychiatrists and theologians. Roman Catholics, Jews, Freudians, and Presbyterians all emerged as versatile and inquiring individuals, not merely as representatives of some fixed notion of what they ought to believe. The various coffee breaks often were as interesting as the formal discussions themselves.

Following the second conference, Dr. Karl requested that the quarterly scientific journal, *Bulletin of the Menninger Clinic*, for November of 1955, be devoted to some of the papers presented at the second conference.

Even though I have been enormously stimulated by all the conferences on psychiatry and religion, I was most intrigued by the "freedom" seminars and even now I find myself thinking about many aspects of them.

Whatever freedom might be, I concluded that it could not be independent of the cultural, economic, physical, or biological worlds. If the body was not healthy, if poverty dominated the scene, or if one had little or no education, the chances of freedom were limited. Even given relief in these areas, freedom is associated with decision making, decision making with responsibility, and responsibility with tension and anxiety.

Some decisions are part of mundane, daily existence but, collectively, they take their toll. Then there are the major decisions about marriage, children, personal affairs, and business. Shall I give up years of seniority and security in my job for a speculative opportunity with great promise? Is it fair to the family? Do I want to take the risk? After years of discontent, shall I seek a divorce, weighing the personal benefit against the possible harm to the children? Shall I place my dear parent in a nursing home? It would be easier for me, but she doesn't want to go. Am I betraying her love for me?

Go a step farther into the rarefied atmosphere of the judge, the doctor, the scientist, the military leader, the head of a large corporation. The judge: do I sentence this man to two to fourteen years or give him a suspended sentence? What can I do for him without undue risk to society? The surgeon: do I amputate the leg or try to save it at the risk of the patient's life? The scientist: do I add my knowledge and support to the development of a new method of destruction that may kill millions of people, or do I dare risk the chance of a scientist of an unfriendly power developing it first? This was Einstein's blockbuster decision when he recommended to President Roosevelt that he proceed with the project leading to the atom bomb. The military leader: look at the dimensions of the Eisenhower decision when he gave the order for D day.

In a more limited but no less dramatic way, the corporation executive lives on the cutting edge of decision making. He has the Board of Directors, his committees, and his staff, but in the final analysis he has to make the decisions that affect the stockholders, the employees, and the public that uses his service or his product. The decision may involve millions of dollars and thousands of employees, or it may involve just one employee who faces a knotty human situation. Does he try once more to rehabilitate a top officer who has become an alcoholic following his wife's death? The officer is a personal friend and a genius at developing new products, but at the present time he is neglecting his work and embarrassing the company. All these difficult questions are part of the price men pay for using freedom to make agonizing decisions. It is both the grandeur and misery of man to be free, and to learn how to be responsible in the exercise of his freedom.

It may appear strange that these reflections on human freedom, stimulated by the Conference of 1955, had so little to say explicitly about either psychiatry or religion. The conference itself did discuss those aspects of freedom that are of greatest concern to psychiatry and to religion. But in doing so, my own general thinking about freedom was affected; and I discovered new facets of freedom in business, personal life, national affairs, etc. When psychiatry and religion get together at a fundamental level, I believe they have contributions that transcend the technical aspects of their respective concerns. From 1956 through 1960 four other conferences on psychiatry and religion were held at the Menninger Foundation. The topics considered were "The Meaning of Human Suffering"; "Healing"; "The Place of Religion in Psychiatric Education"; and "Constructive Aspects of Anxiety." This last topic I found particularly interesting. Anxiety, like pain, is familiar to everyone and fully understood by no one. In the words of Dr. Smiley Blanton: "This demon dwells in all of us. Some of us learn to control him—some of the time. But none of us ever succeeds in eliminating him altogether. Throughout our life he walks one step behind us, and sometimes—especially during the middle years when vitality begins to ebb and problems seem to multiply themselves—he moves close and puts a grim restraining hand on our shoulders. His name? Anxiety."[19] The report of the last conference was edited by Seward Hiltner and Karl Menninger and published in 1963 by Abingdon Press under the title *Constructive Aspects of Anxiety*. The editors were kind enough to dedicate this book "To Edward Gallahue, whose conviction it is that the resources of religion and of psychiatry can be combined to promote human fulfillment and the purposes of God."

It is likely that some small part of the impetus toward improved understanding between psychiatrists and religionists across the country came from Topeka. The time was ripe, and great progress has been made since the first conference in 1954. In that same year the Academy of Religion and Mental Health was born, designed to provide a forum, both nationally and in local areas, for persons of any or no faith to meet and discuss problems with psychiatrists and other members of the mental health team.

Another striking advance was made when, in the early 1960's, the American Medical Association created a Department of Medicine and Religion under Paul B. McCleave. Its basic purpose was "exploring the means whereby members of the medical profession and members of the clergy can co-operate to bring more effective service to the public; to prevent some forms of disabling functional states; and to help in the rehabilitation of some already in need."

In 1963 the new department was asked to offer a program at the opening meeting of the American Medical Association's annual convention. Several thousand physicians heard addresses by Dr. Edward H. Rynearson of the Mayo Clinic, a friend of mine, and the Right Reverend Fulton J. Sheen, formerly Bishop of Rochester. Dr. Rynearson declared that more than 50 percent of the patients in doctors' waiting rooms are there because of the stress and strain of life, and that their ills are of psychological origin. Dr. Rynearson also advocated the intelligent use of religion in relation to illness, quoting Dr. William J. Mayo: "There is a tendency of the time for a group of intellectuals, that is, persons who have been educated beyond their intelligence, to underrate the value of religion as the universal comforter in times of physical or spiritual stress, but to the mass of the people, religion has the same potency that it has had for two thousand years. The sick man needs faith in his physician, but there comes a time when faith in a Higher Power may be necessary to maintain his morale and sustain his emotions."

A recent report of the A.M.A. said that about half the county medical societies in this country have now had discussion programs that included clergy.

In the several conferences on religion and psychiatry and related activities into which I was drawn, I found myself most deeply indebted to the Menninger brothers. They took my proposals seriously; and I am sure that no other group of leaders could have carried the projects through with the skill they demonstrated.

Only through them could we have had such high-level discussions and such important practical results, not least of which is the growing dialogue between religion and psychiatry.

Sometime previously, I had become involved with Dr. Elton Trueblood on a venture that was now maturing rapidly. Dr. Trueblood had been a guest preacher at our church, and following the service I arranged through our minister to meet him. I looked forward to this occasion, because I had read most of his books and had been helped thereby to find my own belief.

Dr. and Mrs. Trueblood accepted an invitation to our home in the afternoon. Our personalities and interests clicked immediately, and we were soon on a first-name basis. I was greatly interested in his knowledge of philosophy and theology, and he was equally interested in the long, tortuous path which I had followed in my own quest. We arranged to meet again, and on this occasion he told me of a dream he had had for a long time. It was to form an organization to breathe new life into the church through the activities of laymen. He also had thought of an appropriate name, "Yokefellow," an adaptation of a term used by Christ in Matthew 11:29.

After Professor Trueblood had outlined his intelligent and comprehensive plans, I asked him what steps were needed to bring his idea to fruition. He said he needed ten directors who would contribute a total of $10,000 with which to rent a house to serve as office and retreat center. On further inquiry I found that, with his wide acquaintances, it would not have been difficult to get the ten men or the $10,000, but that he had been so busy with his teaching, speaking, and writing that he had not found time to put his plan into action.

I somewhat startled him by saying, "Why not start today?" I then called our company attorney, who happened to have some free time and invited us to drop by. Since it was Sunday, we called on him at home, and Elton outlined a very clear conception of his plan with sufficient general information to incorporate "The Yokefellow Associates." Thus in January, 1954, a new order was born.

Elton soon found eight outstanding men, including the president of Earlham College, to join us on the board; and he raised the necessary funds. He then arranged to rent from the College a large, colonial house, which was adjacent to the campus and formerly used as the home of the president of Earlham. The Yokefellow movement advanced so rapidly under Elton Trueblood's leadership that financial assistance from a large foundation and hundreds of individuals was soon forthcoming.

Elton therefore reduced his teaching load at Earlham to one semester each year and organized the Yokefellows into two groups: the Yokefellow Institute to conduct retreats; and the Yokefellow Associates to provide leadership for the movement. He secured an excellent director, Sam Emerick, to head the Institute with a separate Board of Directors and officers.

Elton Trueblood has since started a number of chapters of the Yokefellow Associates, some with their own paid staffs. Other groups, with no retreat facilities, meet in churches, colleges, and even prisons. Two strong Yokefellow movements flourish outside the country, in Canada and in Japan. The movement has continued to blossom and prosper, hundreds of retreats have been held at the headquarters at Richmond alone, and recently, a beautiful $350,000 Yokefellow building was constructed on the Earlham campus.

During these years it seemed that my life consisted mostly of opening doors to new interests. One that particularly delighted me was serving on the Board of Trustees of Butler University. While I had not gone to college there, I had grown up in its atmosphere in Irvington, and most of my friends and social acquaintances were connected with it when I was of college age. Also, I had known the chairman of the board, Mr. Hilton U. Brown, since childhood, when he permitted the children to use the famous Brown Hill with their sleds in winter.

Today Butler has five colleges with a day enrollment of twenty-five hundred. It has students from forty-five states and five foreign countries and thus exerts an influence on a broad geographical scale.

During Goria's period of growing up, I was surprised to see how much children adopt some of the habits of their parents. I soon found that I had to be more careful of my language, for Gloria began to swear now and then without realizing it. Once she was taking a basket full of her little dinosaur models to school (she had made a collection of some fifteen to twenty of them and knew their names and history quite accurately). I asked her if the children would understand her talk about the dinosaurs, and she said, "No, and the damned teacher probably won't either!" Another time, when she was attending Sunday school and had to wait for Dorothy and me, she became impatient and asked her teacher why they didn't close the "damned church" on time.

Once I was taking a walk with Gloria in the neighborhood, and when the frisky dogs that came along kept jumping up on me with their wet paws, I poked at them with my cane. Whereupon she climbed up on our fence and screamed at the top of her voice, "Daddy is mean to dogs!" All in all, though, she was growing up to be a fine, considerate girl with just enough lapses in her behavior to make her normal. Today she is tall, slender, and attractive, and she moves about with the grace of a gazelle. She has light brown hair, brown eyes, a light olive skin, classic features, and a well-formed body. She seems a combination of Dorothy and me in temperament, with my inquisitive mind and Dorothy's bent for the aesthetic and artistic.

The desire to learn certainly applied to Gloria. Before she could read, she memorized the little stories we read to her so well that, as she turned the pages and repeated the story, she gave the impression of reading. I tried to enter into her world as much as possible, and for many years my entrée was reading the same books and discussing them with her. We started a family reading hour in the evenings, beginning with the Oz books, which had been favorites with Dorothy. These proved so popular that we acquired all that were still in print, some thirty volumes.

It was quite a novel experience for me, in contrast to the material I had been reading, to enter into this world of fantasy, and I was fascinated with Frank Baum's assortment of characters. I have since wished that one of them, Professor H. M. (Highly Magnified) Wogglebug, T.E. (Thoroughly Educated), was real, with his assortment of pills for his students. If they had any trouble with their studies, he just gave them a history pill or a math pill, or whatever. I was surprised that author Baum, with his vivid imagination, beat Aldous Huxley's *Brave New World* by a generation in predicting the use of pills for changing human characteristics.

At about this time, Gloria began writing stories herself and insisted that I have one printed for her at the office, copyright and all. It was a cute little story, written when she was eight, entitled "The Star That Would Not Fall." A couple of years later she wrote a play, about twenty minutes long, which the drama teacher produced at school with Gloria in the lead. It never ceased to amaze me how she came alive on a stage. In everyday life she seemed a shade on the quiet side, unless she was with close friends. But on stage she was a true extravert.

While Dorothy, Gloria, and I were enjoying an unusual degree of happiness, the rest of the family was not faring as well. In 1955 Dudley's second marriage ended in divorce. I felt particularly sad about this development; first, because it had happened to my brother, and secondly, because he had worked so hard since childhood for his outstanding business success.

After his divorce, he accepted a request from the head of the Girl Scouts to help improve their recreational facilities in Brown County. He gave them several hundred acres, which provided an ideal site for an artificial lake and camping ground; then he assisted the leaders in organizing a fund drive for the lake and a colony of buildings for the development of group interests. The colony was named the Gallahue Valley Camp in his honor, and it has such virgin beauty that it reminds me of a description from one of James Fenimore Cooper's stories. I am sure that Dudley gained a vast amount of inner satisfaction from this project, though it is but one example of his generosity to other youth groups.

At about this time, I was stunned by a letter from my cousin Jack Teague. I hadn't heard from Jack in years, other than at Christmas and when he married the nurse who had looked after Uncle Ed before his death. He was now divorced, had lost his money in the proceedings, and wished to borrow some. I couldn't believe it. I knew that since Uncle Ed was a wealthy man, Jack must have received a substantial inheritance, and I also knew that he had always been conservative in his financial affairs. Of course, I sent him the amount requested and said that more would be forthcoming if he needed it. Uncle Ed had been a great help in my early years, and besides I had always liked Jack personally.

In a matter of this kind, I thought it best to ask our former manager in Los Angeles what had happened to Jack, rather than ask his brother Donald, since our manager was well acquainted with the family. I soon received a lengthy explanation that Jack and Uncle Ed had been so close for so many years that Jack was completely lost without him, and that Jack's spur-of-the-moment marriage ended in disillusionment. Further I learned that Jack drank more than he should and had completely lost interest in protecting his finances during the divorce and afterward. I deeply regretted that he had not gotten in touch with me sooner, for having gone through a terrific ordeal myself after Mother's death, I might have been able to help him.

Years later, in 1963, I received a wire from Donald saying that Jack had died of a heart attack. He had asked that he be cremated and that his ashes be sent back to Richmond for burial. Immediately I called the undertaker in Richmond and asked him to be sure to tell me when the vase arrived so that I could be present for the services. For some reason, my message was not properly recorded, and when I called back a couple of weeks later, I was chagrined to find that the interment already had taken place without a relative or friend present. I could not help but reflect once more on the curious twists of fate and the tragic end at age sixty of a life so promising. Jack had health, an alert mind, a fine education, a good heritage, and the odds seemed so much more in his favor than mine when we were together on the ranch. Before his divorce he had been quite successful in building houses and developing real estate in Los Angeles, but to my knowledge he had not become the professional writer he hoped to be. I think his life would have been quite different had he secured psychiatric help or pastoral counseling at the right time.

The sands in the hourglass of time were now running out for Father. For years he had continued to call me on the phone every evening and write to me two or three times a week. Retired and alone now, he had no responsibilities and few assets besides Dudley and me: his friends in the home in which he lived, the proprietors of the small stores in the neighborhood, and the firemen in Fire House No. 27, where he was an unofficial "chief." He and the firemen on all shifts became close friends largely because he could still hold up his end of the conversation on a variety of subjects.

He had enjoyed excellent health all of his life, in spite of the early abuses of body and brain, and now that he had abstained for years, he continued to keep active and in good shape. However, in March, 1956, when he was eighty-one, he suffered a heart attack. When the doctor called me, I went immediately to his home, and I rode with him in the ambulance to the hospital. His trust in me was heartrending, because he felt that, since I was with him and he was attended by doctors of my selection, he would be all right. The first night he rallied, and it was hard for me to keep him from talking; the next night he died quietly in his sleep.

Though he had not been an ideal father, I did have a great affection for him, which had grown in recent years. His death, too, caused me to reflect on the ironic fortunes of life. My mother, who did not drink or smoke or have any worldly bad habits, had suffered tragically and died at sixty-five; while Father, who had dissipated so much of his life, maintained good health and died peacefully in his sleep at eighty-one. He had good parents, good connections, good health, and good looks; and after all these years, he left a legacy of an old beat-up typewriter and a trunk full of letters yellowed by time.

Father's funeral was held at the mortuary in Irvington where I had worked nights as a teen-ager. Most of his older friends had passed away, but the younger ones in his neighborhood, along with the firemen from Fire House No. 27, attended his funeral and the interment in the family mausoleum. I appreciated what good friends the firemen were to arrange the time off, and though the setting was different, I'm sure that their fellowship was just as close as that in any club.

On the business front, the tempo was increasing day by day. Fortunately, it was all on the positive side of growth and profits, which nevertheless increased the strain on me, for as fast as I would delegate responsibility for today's problems, tomorrow would produce new growth situations that had to be chewed and digested. The trend of one company writing multiple lines of fire and casualty insurance, indeed, everything but life, was now shifting to include life insurance as well. To keep abreast of this development, I decided to organize a life insurance company as a subsidiary. Fortunately, we had a fine staff to help us, and I was able to entrust the major organizing of the company to one key man, our executive vice-president, John Phelan. He did an excellent job recruiting experienced life insurance personnel to staff the new organization and created an outstanding training program for our branch sales managers. As an added incentive our staff was given liberal ten-year stock options totaling 100,000 shares at the original price paid in by American States, and the next strata of personnel were sold stock at this low price. And in May, 1958, the American States Life Insurance Company was born.

The new venture was a natural for us, since we had almost three thousand agents writing fire and casualty policies, and their policyholders also bought life insurance. It was principally a matter of creating simple forms, rates, and procedure so that our agents could learn the rudiments of selling life insurance easily and back up sales with expert assistance from our field managers on the larger or more complicated cases.

On the underwriting side, we entered into a very desirable reinsurance arrangement with the Lincoln National Life Insurance Company. By sharing our business with them, our limit of loss on any one policy was nominal, and since they bore part of the risk, they were equally interested in our selection of business. In addition, they furnished us a list of doctors whom they already had employed for medical examinations in all the states in which we operated. This gave us blue-ribbon medical assistance that would have taken years to establish ourselves.

Our entry into the life insurance business was so well planned that it started off with flying colors, and the growth and success since have been remarkable. In just a few years the stock appreciated several hundred percent. Another indication of success has been that officers of many other multiple line fire and casualty companies with a life subsidiary have visited our home office over the years to study our program, including officers of some of the great national companies.

With our continued growth, the multiple lines of insurance to sell and service, and the attendant stresses, I was reminded of Socrates' relief of itching by scratching. Of course itching begins again, which starts an endless cycle of itching and scratching.

I felt caught up in an endless cycle of decision making. We had such a vigorous, talented, and ambitious staff of younger men who wanted to spread their wings and fly that it would have been impossible to slow our growth without hurting morale. The growth was stimulating and exciting to them, and it accelerated their careers. The irony of it was that I had devoted my life to creating this *esprit de corps*, and now I was a victim of my own success. Ten years earlier, I should have welcomed this situation as Utopia in business, but now that I was in my late fifties my values had changed.

When young and hungry, I poured my life into achieving business success and the money and recognition that go with it. Now that I had all these things in an even larger measure than I had expected, I realized something of the price I had paid in pressure and tension, which were draining my energy. If I continued in my present mode, the pressures would not only impair my health but narrow my life, like a river that cuts a deeper and narrower channel.

At about this time Edward Auer, a senior officer of Lincoln Life, called on me. He mentioned that Lincoln was thinking seriously of entering the fire and casualty field and acquiring a company, since they felt the trend was toward one organization offering all lines of insurance, just as ours did. In order to do this, it would be necessary to write the fire and casualty lines through a subsidiary, because the insurance laws do not permit one company to write both life *and* fire and casualty insurance.

He then asked me if we might be interested in selling American States. He further stated that Lincoln would have no thought of changing the name of the company or any of the personnel, since it would indeed be helped by retaining the same name and management.

Consideration of the sale of American States to Lincoln did not present the same problems as would have a sale to another fire and casualty company. For in this instance, there would be no merger of departments or dislocation of our management structure, since even our life insurance company was represented by the American States agents. Furthermore, our staff was acquainted with the Lincoln management and had a high respect for it. The only problems left would be the emotional ones for our staff, Dudley, and myself. The staff would go through the disturbing experience of a change in management, but careers would not be affected adversely. As a matter of fact, they might be enhanced since each man would move up a notch if I retired from the company, and since with the Lincoln's financial resources, it could furnish all the capital necessary to expand indefinitely.

Also, because most of the key officers of the company were much younger than I, it was always possible for something to happen to me before their retirement age; in such an event, the American States might be sold to another company under less favorable circumstances, completely upsetting the future of the career personnel. Thus a sale to Lincoln might guarantee most security for our people in the long run than I could guarantee myself.

At this time I told Mr. Auer that Dudley and I couldn't bring ourselves to think of the sale, because we were too emotionally tied to the company. It was a part of our bloodstream. However, in order to relieve some of the tension, we did sell the Agents Finance Company to one of our local banks, the president of which was on our Board of Directors. The sale turned out well for all concerned.

About two years after my first talk with Edward Auer, he again approached me. He said that Lincoln had been observing a number of fire and casualty companies that might be for sale, but before entering into the negotiations he wanted to ask me if we would reconsider selling American States, since they would prefer buying our company because of our outstanding record. We had been successful in making an underwriting profit on our insurance risks for each of the past fifteen years. This record could be matched by very few fire and casualty insurance companies. This time, instead of flatly refusing, I asked him for a few days to think the matter over. I had a hard choice. It was a highly charged emotional problem to consider voluntarily leaving a company that I loved, and yet I couldn't continue indefinitely. If I retired now, it would certainly be better for my health and family. If we were ever going to sell American States, now was the time, since we were at the peak of our efficiency and growth, and the Lincoln offered ideal conditions for our personnel. After reflecting on all aspects of the situation, I decided that, on balance, we should consider a sale to Lincoln. After my decision, I then talked to Dudley and he concurred. After this conversation I told Edward Auer that I was willing to enter into negotiations, the only stipulation being that we should conduct our discussions at my home, so that we could keep the whole matter confidential and avoid the spread of needless rumors.

We soon reached a point in our negotiations where it seemed favorable for the president of Lincoln Life, along with some of their other executives who were specialists in different departments, to be present. However, I continued to represent the American States alone since, fortunately, I was familiar with all aspects of our business. Due to our excellent record of profitable operations, both from the insurance business and investments, our stock was already selling above the price offered for the average fire and casualty company stock. It was now a question of how big a premium we should receive.

Thus my next step was to establish the price and get into the tedious technical process of financial exhibits and legal documents. Following our meeting, a brief, clear, and concise proposition to buy the American States Insurance Company was submitted to me from Lincoln to be presented to our Board of Directors. I then talked to Dudley, and after he reviewed Lincoln's offer his reaction was favorable. We next called a special meeting of our Board of Directors. After I had explained that, in keeping with their loyalty and ability, our career personnel would be taken care of, I presented the Lincoln offer of thirty-six dollars a share, which amounted to an accumulated profit, since the inception of the company, of approximately $26,000,000 for our stockholders. I pointed out that during the past fifteen years each share of stock had increased 24.2 times through stock splits and dividends, and that during this period the dollar value had increased from $30 to $871 a share.

After our board had agreed, unanimously, to submit the offer to the stockholders with their recommendation, I had crossed the Rubicon, and it was now my duty to inform our staff. Unfortunately, they were all in Nassau attending the meeting of our agents who had won a vacation there in one of our prize contests. When our officers had returned, and I had gone through my reasoning step by step, I believe they began to realize that the sale had advantages for them as well as all other parties over the long run.

After covering all matters in detail, I think the staff agreed that the sale was good for all of us financially, that the real problem was the emotional one of terminating our close relationship. The Lincoln's offer was based on buying a minimum of 80 percent of the stock; and when the thirty days were up, over 90 percent of the stock had been tendered. Thus the sale was made official in January, 1963. Dudley and I agreed to stay on a few months to make the transition as smooth as possible.

Later I had a farewell luncheon with all of the members of my Administrative Committee, and I presented each of them with a set of cuff links that I had purchased at Tiffany's. At the end of the meeting, I quoted a verse from Shakespeare's *As You Like It* that seemed appropriate to the occasion:

All the world's a stage,
And all the men and women merely players;
They have their exits and their entrances;
And one man in his time plays many parts,[20]

Indeed, the time had come for me to make my exit from one part and my entrance into another. This last meeting was a sentimental one, since we had developed a close personal fellowship, working for common goals and sharing many personal ups and downs. However, any sadness was tempered by the fact that I would still be in town, and the staff would continue working together with security and a bright future.

All the formalities of my retirement were over now, except for a dinner party with our old directors and the two new members of the board from Lincoln Life. Our attorney, Kurt Pantzer, hosted the party at his lovely home. It was black tie, and Kurt surpassed himself to make it a gala occasion.

As I left Kurt Pantzer's, I thought how fortunate I had been, not just to have achieved respectable status and financial success, but to have known concurrently such warm fellowship. The timing of the sale had been exactly right. It was good for the stock-holders, for the career personnel, for Lincoln, and for me. Driving home that night, I felt curiously exhilarated, because my life had a new dimension and I had a sense of freedom. I thanked God for the past, and I looked forward to the future with a youthful enthusiasm.

Nine

The morning after my retirement, I was having coffee in the library when I seemed to gravitate toward the oil painting of myself and the Borsato figurine on the shelf underneath. It was a striking contrast—the portrait of a well-groomed businessman with a serious, determined expression on his face, and the figurine, an old tramp taking a nap on a bench after apparently drinking too much, his empty beer pail resting beside him. His hat was pushed back off his head, and he had a red nose. His bare knee protruded through a hole in his pants, and his toes were sticking out of his socks. The figurine consummately depicted the epitome of a lazy, indolent, good-for-nothing bum with a don't-give-a-damn attitude. Years ago I had had a flash of insight that here, symbolically, were my two selves. Many times during the stress and strain of business and other pressures that produced nervous tension and frustration, I envied the carefree indolence of the old tramp on the bench. Yet however much I played with the idea, I could never quite settle for the tramp image.

In my bachelor years, I had many interludes of letting myself go in a great variety of activities, but the deep current was always an overpowering drive to succeed, an intellectual desire to learn, and restlessness and yearning for meaning. At times, in my frustration, I would react by almost flying out of orbit, but, just at the outer edge, some power would act as a center of gravity to pull me back. Now that I was retired I shared Karl Menninger's apprehensions about retirement; like him, I reflected on David Neiswanger's searching questions:

If each of us can be helped by science to live a hundred years, what will it profit us if our hates and fears,

our loneliness and our remorse
will not permit us to enjoy them?
What use is an extra year or two
to the man who kills what time he has?[21]

I had no idea what my major future interest would be. I did know that I wanted to continue giving my attention to several outside activities, like the Menninger Foundation, the Methodist Church, hospitals and Butler University, where I had recently been elected chairman of the Gifts and Bequests Committee. However, I decided to take a vacation for the next several months and try to unwind. The time was ideal, since spring was awakening, and I had numerous activities to look forward to with my family and friends.

By the time fall rolled around I moved into my new office, just five minutes from home. My vitality revived, I was ready to carry on with some ideas that had been fermenting for some time. First, I wanted to copy items I had underlined in my books over the years and have them properly indexed. Many times I had wanted to refer to a given passage, but not being a scholar, I usually had trouble finding it. I soon got this project started with my secretary and then turned my thoughts toward two new fields in which I wanted to acquire some basic knowledge.

One was certain areas of science, principally materials on the atom and Einstein's theory of Relativity; and the other, world religions. It might appear on the surface that science and world religions are unrelated, which they are in a strict sense, but in a broader sense both have to do with the world we live in. I first decided to apply myself to the study of the atom.

I already knew something of the atom's composition, which is really like a small solar system with a nucleus that has a positive charge and one or more electrons with a negative charge that whirl around the nucleus at the fantastic speed of seven billion times a second . . . "Whirling around at this tremendous speed, the electron weaves a dense shell all around the nucleus just as a spinning airplane propeller forms a solid disc."[22]

Strangely enough, most of the atom is empty space. "If all

the empty space could be removed from a human body—if all its nuclei and electrons could be crowded together into a solid mass, the body would shrink to the size of a tiny grain of sand that can barely be felt between the tips of our fingers. Or, take 5,000 battleships and aircraft carriers, if all the empty space in their atoms were removed, all these ships could be crowded into the dimensions of a baseball! But this 'baseball' still would weigh as much as all the 5,000 battleships and aircraft carriers."[23]

I was particularly interested in the atom bomb, which is composed of billions of uranium atoms. While its construction is very complicated and sophisticated, the principle of chain reaction is really quite simple. Picture the nucleus of a uranium atom as 238 pellets tightly fused together, which represents 92 protons and 146 neutrons. Then imagine a bullet striking this nucleus, splitting it in two. For a whisper of time, "the two nuclear parts lie side by side, then—because both fragments contain dozens of protons with a positive charge—they repel each other with a giant force and are driven apart in a terrific recoil."[24] At the same time, some neutrons are broken loose and fly away at a fantastic speed. Since they have no charge, they serve as bullets to split other nuclei which, in turn, fly apart, thus setting up an instant chain reaction of billions of atomic fragments that repel each other at such speed that it causes excessive heat—millions of degrees—the heat of atomic fission.

The principle of the atom bomb is based on the energy released when a heavy nucleus comes apart, while the principle of the hydrogen bomb is just the opposite—its energy is released when the light hydrogen nucleus fuses together, as follows: "In exact numbers, 2 protons and 2 neutrons weigh 4.033 atomic weight units. If fused together to form a helium nucleus, they weigh 4.003 units—0.030 weight units less. This amount of mass is transformed into energy every time a helium nucleus is formed from its component parts. Obviously this process holds greater promise of virtually inexhaustible energy than the fission of uranium. Fusion of light elements is what actually happens in the deep core of the sun. This is the secret of solar energy. Fusion of hydrogen nuclei can take place only at temperatures of millions of degrees. Only then do the nuclei move fast enough to break through one another's electric armor, come into contact, and fuse, releasing energy in the process. This is why physicists call such nuclear fusion a 'thermonuclear reaction.'

"It is from such thermonuclear processes that the hydrogen bomb gets its awesome power. In an H-bomb explosion the high temperature necessary is supplied by a normal A-bomb. In the heat of the initial flash, hydrogen fuses in a blast of incredible proportions. Uranium thus becomes only the trigger for the release of more energy than uranium itself could provide."[25]

What impressed me most was learning that all existence depends on the speed of the electrons that produce the shell of the atom. It seemed fantastic to me that the universe and every living thing was dependent for its existence on the speed of a fragile whisper of a particle so infinitesimal, ethereal, and ghostlike that there are no adequate terms to describe it. When I reached this point, I had a horrible thought: What if the electrons should slow down below some unknown toleration point to maintain the atom's shell? All life would be snuffed out instantly, and the entire universe would collapse. It could be slowing down imperceptibly now, and we wouldn't know it, because we haven't observed it long enough. I am no scientist, but how does anyone know that the electrons represent constant, perpetual motion with no friction, loss of energy, or speed through infinity?

At about this time I read a biography of Albert Einstein by Authur Beckhard, which included the account of how the United States secured the formula for splitting the atom, which led to our production of the bomb. In December, 1938, Dr. Otto Hahn and his associate Fritz Strassmann succeeded in splitting a uranium atom in two at the Kaiser Wilhelm Institute of Chemistry in Berlin. They did not have the correct explanation for the phenomenon immediately, but a short time later Otto R. Frisch and Lise Meitner, co-workers of Hahn's, offered the right one—nuclear fission. Miss Meitner realized that a set of chain reactions could be set up, a series of explosions as each unity of energy was released, each explosion many times bigger than the one before it.

At this point, she learned that she was in immediate danger of being seized by the Gestapo and put in a concentration camp because she was Jewish, a classic example of the stupidity of hate groups. It was indeed ironic that the Nazis were persecuting a scientist who had just discovered the formula for producing an atom bomb, with which Germany might have conquered and ruled the world. With the help of co-workers, she barely escaped to Denmark, where she sought out a leading fellow scientist, Dr. Nils Bohr. He, in turn, smuggled her notes to Dr. Fermi, who was working at Columbia University with another great scientist, Dr. Szilard. These two later arranged a meeting with Dr. Einstein at his home in Princeton. The unpretentious garden at the rear of Einstein's modest, white frame house thus became the focal point for one of the most dramatic moments in the world's history. After a briefing by Drs. Fermi and Szilard, Dr. Einstein wrote his famous letter to Franklin Roosevelt on August 2, 1939, which led to the Manhattan Project and the atom bomb.

I could not help but wonder if humanity wouldn't have been better off if the United States had used the monopoly of the atom bomb to rule the world. I know that ethics are against it, but, in the light of our experiences in the last twenty years, good judgment would be for it. It is not the nature of the American nation to rule as an inhuman despot, and, at one stroke, we could have eliminated the colossal waste of military budgets for all countries and devoted this time and energy to eliminating poverty the world over. In turn, some acceptable form of home rule could have been established for all nations, and we would be living in a world with some semblance of cooperation instead of a balance of terror.

I wonder if future historians will look back on this period of United States monopoly of the bomb and say with deep regret: Once upon a time, the United States could have wiped out war for all time, and the human family could have learned to live together. But the United States was too immature and idealistic to realize that the end justified the means, although we did not have this compunction in connection with the American Indians, whose country we conquered, relegating their members to poverty-stricken reservations. Instead of taking a strong position, in a few years we were allies of our former enemies and enemies of our former allies, with the world on the brink of disaster. I am truly inclined to believe that future historians may well think that we were more naïve than good and did not fulfill our destiny.

The biography of Albert Einstein also aroused my interest in the Theory of Relativity. I had read a few books on astronomy, but I had no specific knowledge of the Theory of Relativity. I felt that the best starting point was a talk with the head of the Math Department at Butler University. He recommended two books to me that were also recommended by Dr. Einstein: *The Universe and Dr. Einstein* by Lincoln Barnett and *Relativity for the Layman* by James A. Coleman.

I was immediately impressed with the incredible complexity, number, and speed of objects in space. Starting with our own solar system, the earth rotates on its axis at the rate of a thousand miles an hour, and on its annual revolution around the sun at a rate of a million and a half miles a day. "The entire solar system, moreover, is moving within the local star system at the rate of one million miles a day; and the whole Milky Way is drifting with respect to the remote external galaxies at the rate of seven and one-half million miles a day—and all in different directions!"[26] Add to this the billions of other galaxies wheeling and racing away from each other, each containing internal movements of spinning local solar systems and whirling star systems, and one gets some idea of the activity of celestial bodies.

This turned my thoughts to the relativity of position. While I sit at my desk, I remain on the same spot on earth, but while I'm writing this sentence, I have changed my position relative to every other object in space, as the earth and every object in space has moved. From this simple illustration, it is obvious that the location of any celestial body is subject to the reference point and the time of the observer. Thus time becomes a fourth dimension, and it is meaningless to talk about the location of any celestial body without knowing the time. Time alone is also meaningless unless we know the reference point of the observer.

Another aspect of relativity is that of the phenomenon of motion, of which Barnett gives a clear, simple example, as follows: "Anyone who has ever ridden on a railroad train knows how rapidly another train flashes by when it is traveling in the opposite direction, and conversely how it may look almost motionless when it is moving in the same direction. A variation of this effect can be very deceptive in an enclosed station like Grand Central Terminal in New York. Once in a while a train gets under way so gently that passengers feel no recoil whatever. Then if they happen to look out the window and see another train slide past on the next track, they have no way of knowing which train is in motion and which is at rest; nor can they tell how fast either one is moving or in what direction. The only way they can judge their situation is by looking out on the other side of the car for some fixed body of reference like the station platform or a signal light."[27] A more sophisticated illustration would be: ". . . If all the objects in the universe were removed save one, then no one could say whether that one remaining object was at rest or hurtling through the void at 100,000 miles a second. Motion is a relative state; unless there is some system of reference to which it may be compared, it is meaningless to speak of the motion of a single body."[28]

One of the most interesting concepts of relativity has to do with velocity. All sorts of strange occurrences take place as objects reach a high degree of velocity, reaching that of light, 186,282 miles a second, the top limiting velocity in the universe. Clocks slow down as velocity increases and would stop all together if they reached the velocity of light. Even the heart and aging process would slow down in a human being with high acceleration. If a bullet reached the velocity of 90 percent of light, it would contract to half in size, but increase its mass.

I studied many other aspects of the Theory of Relativity, which helped me to understand the world we live in. I think it is better for a novice in any field to try to broaden his interests than to confine himself to his own specialty, where he excels in prestige while shutting himself off from knowledge of the rest of the world. Einstein's thoughts on this subject are well worth repeating: "It is of great importance that the general public be given an opportunity to experience—consciously and intelligently—the efforts and results of scientific research . . . Restricting the body of knowledge to a small group deadens the philosophical spirit of a people and leads to spiritual poverty."[29]

After my little look-in at science, I secured two good books as starting points on world religions: *The World's Living Religions* by Robert E. Hume, the great scholar from Union Theological Seminary, and *The Great Religions of the Modern World*, a symposium by a number of leading scholars, edited by Edward Jurji of Princeton Theological Seminary. I had no idea how exciting this quest could be. Most of the non-Christian religions had always been shrouded in mystery to me, with their distinctive cultures, strange rites, and curious customs. But when I got involved in the subject, I found that the rituals, rites, and customs are only veneer, and that the history and basic principles are not difficult to understand. A whole new world opened to me, embracing all the ideas man has ever thought, dreamed or conjured up.

Strangely enough, some of the most foreign religions have had the profoundest effect on our Christian beliefs, yet if you were to ask the man in the street what he thought of Zoroaster, he probably would tell you he had never heard of him. However, the ideas of Zoroaster, a Persian born in 660 B.C., form the roots of many ideas that the twentieth-century Christian holds sacred. During the period of Persian power, Zoroastrianism was most influential, and had a fascinating influence on the Hebrew and Christian religions and a closer connection with the Bible than any other religion. During the Babylonian captivity, the Jews were in direct contact with this religion, and kings of Persia are mentioned in numerous books of the Bible. During captivity, the Jews absorbed many of the ideas of Zoroastrianism and grafted them onto their own religion. It is responsible for the use of the words "Satan" and "Paradise" in the Bible, the idea of a hierarchy of angels and demons, as well as a great Savior to come, and a final Resurrection and Judgment, whereby the righteous are sent to Heaven, the wicked sent to Hell.

As I probed deeper into the non-Christian religions, I became greatly interested in their origin, theology, and history. Virgin births, miracles, monastic orders, and a high code of ethics are sprinkled throughout, so it seems only reasonable to assume that some of these ideas were also adopted by the Jews and Christians. While any one of the major religions could probably occupy scholars for a lifetime, their bare-bone essentials can be summarized.

Islam was founded by Muhammad (570–632). The Moslems consider him the latest and greatest prophet to receive revelations from God. The sacred scripture of Islam is the Koran, but Jewish and Christian writings are respected, and Jesus is regarded as a major prophet. On the positive side, I was impressed by the monotheism of Islam, very similar to that of Judaism, by Islam's insistence on a life of daily prayer, and by its rejection of racial discrimination. On the other side, however, I could neither admire nor condone the view of the Koran as infallible, the emphasis on force and violence under various conditions, the apparently literal ideas about a future life, and the fact that no fundamental provision seems to be made for rethinking the faith in the light of changing conditions, as is done in Christianity.

Hinduism dates back to about 1500 B.C. and is the oldest organized religion in the world. It is a complete outgrowth of a very devout people with many different temperaments. It has been diversified and yet unified by its theoretical belief in one immanent, all-inclusive, impersonal World Soul (Brahma) and by its social control through caste. It involves a denial of God's personality and tends to identify God with nature, which has led to the worship of many minor gods and objects of nature. Its caste system was originally divided into four classes, but is now divided into hundreds of subcastes. It believes in the transmigration of souls, and there is supposed to exist an impersonal cosmic power of justice that administers just retribution to every person according to his deeds, assigning him to a higher or lower caste in his next reincarnation. If a person has been unusually good, he may escape earthly reincarnation altogether and ascend to a supreme state of impersonality.

When I examined Buddhism, I found it the most complex and baffling of all the non-Christian religions. It has assumed so many forms, and has been divided into so many groups, such as Zen, Hinayana, and Mahayana, that only a scholar can fathom its wide range of ideas. Thus, every time I thought I had nailed down its central meaning, I'd come upon some Buddhist group to question it. In Gautama, the founder of Buddhism, I found much to admire. Born in the sixth century before Christ, son of a Hindu nobleman, he had an experience in his late twenties that took him away from being the complacent heir to wealth and set him on a path of ethical leadership. Seeing an old man, a sick man, and a corpse, and a religious ascetic oblivious to their suffering, Gautama decided he could not be indifferent to human suffering. He decided to dedicate his life to self-sacrifice and a search for peace. He even renounced his family in order to pursue his quest. The problem of suffering was Gautama's preoccupation.

Suffering, Gautama decided, came from indulging desires. If the desires themselves could be suppressed or kept in balance, then suffering could be decreased or eliminated. Man must think of desire in every aspect; and when he does, he may learn kindness, aspiration, right belief, right speech, action, thought, and concentration. Gautama rejected the caste system in India, but retained belief in the transmigration of souls.

Jainism, a reform movement of Hinduism, was founded in India shortly before Buddhism. Its founder, Mahavira, advocated a humble and ascetic system of moral self-discipline. He protested the hierarchy of caste, but his followers were never successful in eliminating it.

Sikhism also came out of India and is the most recent of the world's great religions. In the fifteenth century of our era, Nanak, its creator and a contemporary of Martin Luther, left his family for religious contemplation and eventually announced, "There is no Hindu and no Musalman." By this he meant that those elements of Hinduism and Islam that he regarded as valid could and should be combined. Like Gautama, he advocated elimination of the caste system, but retained belief in the transmigration of souls.

I began to see that as a Western Christian trying to get my bearings with the religions founded in India, I always came back to the question of whether they were religions as I understood religion. I began to see in a new way why there is no word, in most of the Oriental languages, for "religion." When I turned to the religions of Chinese origin, my question was the same.

I tried next to seek out the rudiments of Confucianism. Confucius lived in the fifth and sixth centuries B.C., had to work hard as a boy, married and had a family. He was a successful teacher at an early age and served as chief justice of his state until ousted by some political intrigue. Refusing to become disillusioned, he continued to campaign for political reforms. He wrote and taught for the remainder of his long life, but at his death he was a disappointed old man.

To a Western eye, Confucius was more like Benjamin Franklin than like either Jesus or Paul. Can a religious faith be based on witty epigrams and sayings, no matter how wise? Confucius stressed the importance of strong family ties and consequent duty, love, and reverence for parents. Unhappily to me, this often turned into ancestor worship, thus into a further denial of the needs of the living human person. Confucius discouraged prayer or any other form of concern for the supernatural. I was impressed with the wisdom of Confucius—but can there be any religion without God, without prayer?

Taoism is also of Chinese origin. Little is known of its founder, Lao-tze, who was born forty-four years before Confucius in 604 B.C. He held a high government post, but found time for both contemplation and writing. His writing concerned his search for the "Tao," or the Way. This was the principle of the universe and of life. Like everything Chinese, it combined the practical and theoretical. Lao-tze's *Tao-Te-Ching*, or *Canon of Reason and Virtue*, tells of one eternal and impersonal Supreme Being with whom mystical contact is possible. It also contains much excellent ethical teaching, with a wisdom rivaling that of the ancient Jews and in much the same spirit of doing good to others. For me the trouble with Taoism was its heavy emphasis on mysticism, which has little effect on concrete evils of human existence.

Shintoism is the formalization of indigenous Japanese religion. This formalization took place as a reaction to the importation of Buddhism into Japan. For this reason, Shintoism has been related to the distinctive character of Japan and to the royal household. Before World War II Shintoism was divided into two cults, state Shinto and shrine Shinto. It was the cult of state

Shinto that was abolished by the American Occupation authorities in 1945, when Emperor Hirohito declared, "The Emperor is not a living god."

Shrine Shinto continues. Coexistent with Japanese history, Shinto until recently held that the Japanese islands were the first instance of divine creation and that the first Mikado was a lineal descendant of the sun goddess. Thus each succeeding ruler shared in the divine inheritance. Shinto's sacred scriptures contain poems, legends, and accounts of the nation's divine origin. But they are almost devoid of struggles with good and evil, questions of social justice, or the mysteries of a life eternal.

I have never ceased to wonder why all the major religions originated in the East. So far as there is an answer, beyond Eastern civilization preceding the West's, it seems to lie in the *character* of Oriental and Near East peoples. To this day, they are ascetic, subjective, intuitive, mystical, and impressionistic, having the stuff of which dreams and revelations are made, while the dominant characteristics of the West are action, power, scientific investigation, acquisitive materialism, and the faith to change the world, the stuff of which dynamic leadership is made.

I was struck by factors of time as well as place. Six of the eleven religions I had reviewed originated in a period of 109 years, from 660 B.C. to 551 B.C. This same period saw the activities of the great Hebrew prophets, Jeremiah, Isaiah of the Exile, and Ezekiel. It also was the period of five of the famous early Greek philosophers: Thales, Anaximander, Anaximenes, Xenophanes, and Pythagoras. In all human history, that century was the most notable for the search for meaning.

I now read some of the scholars who had attempted to consider the whole history of the world's religions. I wanted to find out whether the great religions of the world could update themselves sufficiently to be an integral part of the modern world yet properly critical of it, and whether they could in some way understand one another enough to get along together and help the world that is emerging to find its values on a high plane, valuing but transcending material affairs. I have found that some of the Western scholars have asked similar questions.

Arnold J. Toynbee believes that the impact of Western civilization upon the rest of the world reached its peak in our century, for good or ill. Will we in the West, he asks, give the historian of the year A.D. 3047 any ground for saying that, conversely, the West became alert and began to listen to the rest of the world?

In *The Coming World Civilization*, William Ernest Hocking declared that there is an inherent universalism in religions and that especially the people of any religion with mystical tendencies find it easy to understand their counterparts in other religions. Hocking felt that the world is in the process of "unsteadily merging" into a single world civilization; he obviously believed that this would be desirable if it could be managed.

Hendrik Kramer, in *World Cultures and World Religions*, suggests that the Orient and Occident have met in the last century and a half in a way unknown to previous ages, but that this meeting has only begun. Up to this time, meeting has been because it could not be helped. The "play," therefore, is only now in process of being "staged," in the sense that the meeting is being mutually desired and diligently pursued. Kramer knows that Christians must listen to the Oriental religions as well as try to speak to them.

Reflecting on what I had read, it seemed to me that it had been the religions of the world that had given man his sense of meaning and purpose. Granted the great variety among them, the division within them, the perversion of holy wars, fiendish persecution, and much mutual hostility and hypocrisy through the ages, was it possible for them to rise to the challenge of the new age, understand one another more adequately and appreciatively, and thus, more than ever before, guide man in his constructive use of new discoveries as well as in his age-old quest for meaning? From my recent studies of science, I had concluded that scientific advance and the technologies flowing from it do indeed promise great things for man's future, if only he can avoid destroying himself.

How, I wondered, could I have some part in this moral movement? I decided to begin by contacting my friend, Dr. Seward Hiltner, Professor of Theology and Personality at Princeton Theological Seminary. I had known Dr. Hiltner for several years, since he had served as a visiting consultant at the Menninger Foundation and had taken a leading part in all the conferences I had sponsored there in religion and psychiatry. I told Dr. Hiltner that I would like to finance and sponsor a conference on world religions at Princeton if Dr. James McCord, the Seminary president, were interested. He then approached Dr. McCord, who said he was making a trip west shortly and would arrange to include Indianapolis in his schedule and visit with me. Our first meeting took place early in 1963, and I was greatly impressed by Dr. McCord's vision and knowledge in world religions. He was familiar with and attracted by the views of Toynbee, Hocking, Kramer, and many other scholars, all pointing to the importance of a better understanding among the world's religions.

Dr. McCord offered to take up my suggestion with Dr. Jurji, Professor of History of Religions, and other members of the faculty and Board of Trustees, and if the action was favorable, he would ask Dr. Jurji to prepare an outline of his ideas for such a conference I later heard from Dr. McCord, who said that Princeton would undertake the conference if it could do something significant on a high-level basis. I then received a tentative outline and budget from Dr. Jurji suggesting two conferences—the first to be attended by leading American scholars, the second leading scholars from abroad representing Mohammedanism, Buddhism, and Hinduism, along with informed Americans representing Christianity and Judaism.

Dr. Jurji went on to say that the first conference should be limited to forty or fifty people and should be long enough to permit discussion in depth. In addition, it should be carried on, he said, in a spirit of respect for each person's religious conviction and with an openness to criticism on all sides. He added: "Underlying the project is an awareness that a chief purpose of our time is to learn and to prove that science and faith, culture, and theology can live together, since at least at certain points they are compatible. Strangely enough, the differences of type among the world's religions are dwarfed in comparison with an almost unbridgeable chasm between, on the one hand, all the religions, and on the other, those so-called quasi-religions, Facism,

Communism, liberal humanism, and scientism—offshoots of secularism."

After reading Dr. Jurji's outline, I became quite excited about the project and cheerfully agreed to sponsor and finance the two conferences. In order to conduct the two conferences in an appropriate way and get the best possible representatives from the Orient, the Near East, and Europe, I proposed to Dr. McCord that Dr. Jurji visit leading scholars all over the world, ascertain their interest, and explain the intent of our conferences in advance. Dr. and Mrs. Jurji spent three months on such a trip in the summer of 1963, a year before the first conference was held. Thanks to this excellent planning, it was possible to begin arranging the 1966 meeting even before the session of 1964 had been held.

The first World Religions Conference convened at Princeton on October 27, 1964. Its theme: "The Phenomenon of Convergence and the Course of Prejudice." In the foreword to the published papers (Supplement to the *Graduate Journal* of University of Texas, VII, 1966), James I. McCord and Edward J. Jurji interpreted that theme: "This is an era in which mankind is at once intimately united and deeply divided. Space and time have been shrunk by the effects of technology, until the problems of the remotest region are the concerns of the entire world. Communities that formerly were isolated now are caught up in the movements of universal history, and strange and alien cultural traditions now confront one another at every hand. But these diverse traditions, accustomed to a life of relative independence and autonomy, have not yet found a way to exist together in integrity and in harmony. Thus there has taken place a magnification of age-old phenomena of prejudice, which continues to thwart community and to produce cultural retardation."

We had fifty scholars from front-rank universities and graduate schools, representing theology, philosophy, psychology, history, and anthropology. There were also distinguished guests like Clarence Faust, vice-president of the Ford Foundation. I think that a consensus ran through the conference, summarized by Dr. Loos: ". . . that revolution—seething, surging—is today digging into the entrails of nearly every society in the world. The revolution is social, political, racial and cultural, economic, technical, moral and spiritual—confirming that we are in a time of troubles, because the old order changes, and because the new order is not yet in place."

Hence the acute need for authentic dialogue between the world religions, the necessity for their learning to live together with some unity in diversity. As Dr. S. Radhakrishnan, President of India, stated: "It is one of the major tragedies of the world that the great religions instead of uniting mankind in mutual understanding and goodwill, divide mankind by their dogmatic claims and prejudices. They affirm that religious truth is attained in this or that special region, by this or that chosen race, condemning others either to borrow from it or else suffer spiritual destitution."

He added that the voice of God reached the spirit of man in a diversity of ways, in a multiplicity of languages, and that religious faith, like life itself, is never final, never an arrival, but rather an endless pilgrimage, a being on the way; and that the all-inclusiveness of God contradicts the exclusiveness of any particular religion.

In the fall of 1964 after the conference at Princeton, I was fortunate in launching an idea at Butler University which I had mentioned to the Board of Trustees on several occasions: a lecture-a-year series by world-renowned persons in various fields. The chairman of the board suggested a title that fitted the idea perfectly, "The Achievements of Man." My first choice for the initial lecture was Dr. Wernher von Braun, and fortunately, through the efforts of our Congressman, Richard L. Roudebush, a leader on the Congressional Committee of space, we succeeded in getting him for our opening lecture at Clowes Hall. The Hall is a beautiful $4,000,000 theater seating 2,200 and was named by *Fortune* magazine one of the ten outstanding buildings to be erected in the United States in 1963. Since that time, it has had an outstanding program of attractions from the United States and abroad.

When Dorothy and I met Dr. von Braun at the airport, he was accompanied by his lovely thirteen-year-old daughter Margrit and his public relations manager, Mr. Jackson. He was only fifty-three, and I had expected him to be much older; he also had an extremely cordial, outgoing personality, and I had expected him to be more formal and reserved. Dorothy and I spent one of the most fascinating hours of our lives at dinner, and I could easily have spent the rest of the evening just asking him questions about science.

He gave an excellent lecture on education and space exploration, emphasizing the need for a broad foundation in basic subjects to educate the whole man and, above all, teaching him how to learn. He said he felt that if a student didn't learn how to learn, especially in the scientific and technological fields, he would be hopelessly obsolete ten years after he got out of school, no matter how good his grades. He then described an imaginary trip to the moon, graphically illustrated with slides on a large screen. Our actual landing on the moon was carried out precisely as he predicted. Dr. von Braun is a genius not only in science, but in his ability to explain technical scientific data so that laymen can understand it.

After the lecture, we attended a reception for him at the home of the president of Butler; it was limited to a small group of trustees and prominent friends of the university. As I watched all these animated people, I couldn't help but think about the house itself, which had once been my own home. I thought about all that had transpired there, first with Mother and later when I lived alone. Life in the house had been kaleidoscopic, embracing the heights of happiness and the depths of despair, the profound and the foolish, frenetic activity and abject loneliness. Now it had come into balance with a university president and a fine family; and all in all, I was glad I had built it and proud that it was used for the present purpose.

After Dr. von Braun's visit, Dorothy and I went to New York to review with Dr. McCord plans for the second World Religions Conference to be held at Princeton in May, 1966. We settled on the theme "Religious Pluralism and World Community."

It was one of the most exciting days of my life when Dorothy and I were met at the Berkshire Hotel in New York City for our drive down to Princeton. Throughout the eight days of the conference, the spring weather was perfect. Most of our meetings were held at the superb Princeton Inn, which is only a block from the Seminary.

Besides eighteen world-renowned scholars from ten foreign countries, the conference registered a list of equally impressive American scholars from Princeton, Harvard, Yale, Dartmouth, Massachusetts Institute of Technology, Fordham, Syracuse, the University of Chicago, the University of California at Los Angeles, and the Jewish Theological Seminary of America. Moreover, two of the Roman Catholic participants were from the newly created Vatican Secretariats for Non-Believers and for Non-Christians.

Since our funds were not, after all, unlimited, the overseas conference membership was concentrated on the three largest and most influential groups, namely, Buddhism, Hinduism, and Islam. But we also had competent scholars who were experts in such other faiths as Taoism and Confucianism. As Edward J. Jurji indicated in his opening statement, this was one of the most representative assemblies of religious scholars ever held.

I was more sure than ever that, in the long run, it is ideas and convictions, rather than material forces, that shape the world. While the subjects discussed at the conference were many and diverse, four points struck me most forcibly:

1. "That man's consciousness of Time may be the origin of all religions." He knows that he has been, that he now is, and that he will be—but for how long? His knowledge of time creates anxiety, apprehension, and fear of the future, the aging process, and death. Thus, religion may be the expression of man's instinctive quest for security, which results from a sense of insecurity caused by his consciousness of Time.

2. No major religion with a closed system of scripture, theology, and dogma can remain a vital force for long in the future. For a religion to remain meaningful, and stay alive, it must be open enough to consider the facts of science as they are discovered. I don't think any religion can survive that espouses statements, creeds, and conclusions drawn centuries ago in a period of complete ignorance of modern science that are clearly false in the light of present scientific fact. After the falsehoods and myths are swept away, the core of the major religions is still there—the great

moral lessons and a God of love, truth, and justice. We must also realize that God did not restrict His revelations to past ages and then shut Himself off from humanity and go into hiding. He is just as close to every faith, every community, and every person as He ever was.

3. An understanding of the religion of a people is indispensable to understanding them culturally, economically, and politically. Therefore any thoughtful understanding of communications across barriers of nation, culture, economics, or race must consider the religious factors. When decisions are made in Washington, London, Paris, Moscow, or at the United Nations regarding how to deal with any country, religious values must be taken into account, besides all the known political, economic, social, and historical factors. Religions of the world are not merely recondite antiquities of concern only to scholars. They are basic facts of the new international life.

4. If the major religions of the world learn to cooperate on some basic points, no matter what their disagreements on other points, the potential benefits to mankind are incalculable. Besides the religious wars of past ages, we have seen warfare in our own generation caused by religious differences. In addition to releasing the tensions causing actual warfare, the major religions could launch a giant cooperative effort in all areas that plague mankind.

The chances of cooperation on some basic points seemed greater after the Princeton conference than I had realized. For instance, H. C. Ganguli, a Hindu from the University of New Delhi, surveyed the views of the great world religions on birth control and contraception and concluded that all favor the principle of limitation and spacing of births according to the capacity of parents to give their children proper nurture, affection, and education; that is, to have children who are wanted and who can be cared for. Further, Ganguli indicated that the one remaining problem confronting a possible worldwide effort at population control was the attitude of the Roman Catholic Church about the method—but not the goal—of such control.

The Roman Catholic hierarchy is now restudying this problem in the light of present conditions, and should it decide to broaden its position on method, it would transform the entire free world.

As matters now stand, members of religions not restricted on birth control are afraid to practice it for fear of losing their relative position of power by being outbred by the Roman Catholics. As a specific case in point, Dr. Jayatilleke, a leading Buddhist and professor of philosophy at the University of Ceylon, told me that the practice of birth control among the Buddhists in Ceylon would be greatly accelerated if the Roman Catholics changed their position. In India, though the Roman Catholic religion does not occupy a major position, the Moslems do, and they are very conscious of the Roman Catholic position which affects their actions throughout Islam.

Think of it. Suppose that the religions of the world—not its nations—should come out with a unified program about population control! This does not seem a wholly remote possibility.

My illustration of birth control has been only one example of a basic point, although an important one to which the conference itself gave special attention. But there are others. And if the hurdle here or there could be jumped, then the religions of the world might very well make more contributions to man's moral and religious progress, on a collective basis, than they have so far been able to do individually.

I enjoyed my private conversations with conference members as much as the official discussions. Since I was so plainly a businessman and not a scholar, nearly every participant finally got round to asking me how I had become interested in world religions, especially since there are only a few hundred scholars of the subject on the entire planet. I told them I had evidently been born with a native curiosity about the mysteries of man, his purpose, and his ultimate destiny, and that I believed that the universal religions, not just Christianity and Judaism, tried to find answers to those questions. I also suggested that their subject of scholarly inquiry had great practical significance for the future of mankind.

When it was time to say farewell, there was not the usual sense of haste that marks a meeting that is breaking up. Instead, there seemed to be a reluctance to say good-bye, because we had developed a wonderful fellowship, working on a common ground for uncommon goals.

The press notices that appeared concerning the conference were deceptively simple. For instance, one piece probably meant very little to most readers of the New York *Times*, but for me it represented a true climax. It brought together the strands of my life in one simple design. It involved my increasing interest in the philosophy of civilization, it expressed my long-felt conviction that the representatives of all religions, though tragically divided, could unite in the same profound quest; it made me grateful that my business success provided the money to make the conference possible. Suddenly, at Princeton, my life as the organizer of a business, as an amateur theologian, a voracious reader, and an inveterate seeker became one.

After my return home from Princeton, I had abundant time to meditate on what I had learned. I was grateful for the fellowship of fifty of the leading religious thinkers of the world. I was also grateful when I received a letter from Father Don Vincenzo Miano of Rome, who represented the Vatican Secretariat for Non-Believers, who stated that he had informed Pope Paul VI directly what had transpired at Princeton, and as a result, I received a silver medal from Pope Paul with the following inscription:

"MANVS TVA DEDVCET ME"
(Your hand leads me)

Ten

Although I had known for some time about a small group of radical theologians who classified themselves as Christian Atheists, I did not begin studying the "Death of God" movement in depth until after the first World Religions Conference at Princeton. Thomas J. J. Altizer was present at that meeting and, though I did not talk with him personally, my interest was caught through discussion of his views by some of the other theologians present.

By the time several national magazines began to pay attention to the "Death of God" movement, I had already done a good deal of reading about it. *Time* devoted a cover to it and subsequently has carried many stories. College newspapers throughout the country have featured articles about it. Considerable attention has been accorded it by *Playboy* magazine, of all unexpected places.

The more I read about this movement and the impact it seemed to be having, the more I became disturbed about the effects it might have on impressionable minds lacking the mental equipment to analyze it properly. For the movement is more complex and subtle than the slogans imply.

I was further intrigued with the question of atheism through the discussions of the two World Religions Conferences. Especially through contact with the Buddhist and Hindu scholars at the second meeting, I had been impressed with the nobility of those faiths, even though they set aside any conception of a personal God.

Impelled by these twin interests, I began to study atheisms, and there seemed to be two basic types. First, there was the kind I had encountered in the scholars of Buddhism and Hinduism.

They thought of themselves in terms of what, positively, they believed, not as atheists; it was only in their encounter with religions like Islam or Christianity that they saw themselves, comparatively speaking, as atheistic. Perhaps, I thought, Socrates and Plato were a bit like that too. In this form of atheism, a person or a group has built up its religion and philosophy and ethics without reference to a personal God, no matter what the reason. This might be called "spontaneous atheism" in that it developed indigenously and was not a reaction to something else.

The other type, however, might be called "reactive atheism." The atheism of Karl Marx and of the Communist movement clearly seemed to be a reaction against what they felt God had meant in the cultures of western Europe and of Russia. Similarly, Friedrich Nietzsche, reared in a Christian culture, was reacting against something when he declared God to be dead.

Since I had had contact with psychiatry for many years, I knew that Freud had been an atheist, though he regarded this as a personal position and did not impose it on his disciples. Freud's principal argument was developmental in form. At first the small child looks at his father or his parents as all-powerful. Gradually he learns to relinquish these mistaken notions of parental power. But he retains a "father image" *even* while slowly detaching it from his real father. He then "projects" this father image onto God. Thus he feels protected in the face of the terrors of the universe. But if he really grows up and faces the terror that the universe does contain, Freud implied, then he will not be under compulsion to believe in God, who is simply a projection of human wishes. Clearly Freud was not only reacting against the Jewish conception of God, but also the forms of belief which he saw in his practice.

Next I reflected that the reactive atheists are bound to be disillusioned in some sense, whether they realize it or not. Both as groups and as individuals, they had once held, or been tempted to hold, beliefs and ideals and convictions which now, whatever the reason, seemed untenable. They now regarded those beliefs as illusions; hence the apt word is "disillusionment."

By this time I felt that I was on the road to understanding the dynamics of the atheisms of the radical theologians.

When I read the three men now identified as the leaders in radical theology—Paul Van Buren, William Hamilton, and Thomas J. J. Altizer—all of them appeared to be disillusioned. I refer of course to their ideas and beliefs and not to their personalities. At first glance, their attitudes toward disillusionment seemed constructive. That is, they were trying to be honest with themselves and others, they were continuing their inquiry into meaning, and they were not settling back into comfortable atheism or agnosticism.

Paul Van Buren is one of the clearest and most direct thinkers among the radical theologians. A student of Karl Barth, perhaps the foremost Protestant theologian of our century, Van Buren seems to me always courageous, always following where his logic leads him, yet always a little sorry that his logic had to lead him from the position he once held. I can find no bitterness in Van Buren, but I think some part of him longs for the old beliefs, though he writes in logical and not in emotional ways, and therefore admits no such thing.

As I read Van Buren I wondered, as I had often wondered while studying philosophy, whether any man can live every dimension of his own life on the basis of logic alone. I do not want a philosopher or theologian to be dishonest, to ignore his own logic, or to tolerate logical contradictions. But when logic seems to lead away from the larger dimensions of one's experience, and even at times from common sense, isn't there a kind of obsessive preoccupation in sticking with logic alone? Although I found myself admiring Paul Van Buren, he appeared to be the greatest victim of his own logic.

When I turned to William Hamilton, the atmosphere was entirely different. Here was the same Van Buren honesty, but there was also more emotional language and wistfulness. In most of his recent writings, Hamilton takes the reader into *every* stage of his intellectual struggle. It is worth noting that Hamilton had been publishing competent theological books and articles for several years before he began to have second thoughts about God. He certainly has the courage of his convictions; for I understand he recently resigned his professorship in a theological seminary to take a position in a liberal arts college.

When I read the third radical theologian, Thomas J. J. Altizer, I found myself confused; although part of this effect may be due to the bombast and lack of clarity of his style, more comes from the content itself. Altizer is the advocate of the notion that "God is dead," and he means specifically that God died with Jesus on the cross. Like Hamilton and Van Buren, Altizer is for our taking Jesus seriously and following him. But he alone among the three declares that God died when Jesus did. Thus he alone seems to say that God, all of God, was in time, and died in time, and thus left time—and so "died."

This argument seems to me incredible. Unless I miss Altizer's point, following it would mean that the God who created the universe saw fit to come to our planet (a speck of dust in one of the millions of galaxies), and then committed suicide through one of his creatures, thus deserting not only man but also the entire universe.

The term "Christian atheism" comes from Altizer. He argues that we should believe in Jesus Christ, but not in God. To me, this is a contradiction in terms.

When I began to read the comments of other theologians about the radical theologians, I saw that my reflections had to include two dimensions. On the one hand, I realized that the positions of these men are extreme and are so regarded by other theologians. On the other, I saw that, even in their extreme way, these men and their positions are part of a much larger and mostly unheralded movement to update Christian theology. And this larger movement is extremely important.

From the time I reached that conviction, I became less concerned about the positions of the radical theologians as such and more concerned with the general movements in theology. And yet, because it has caught the public eye as has no other theological movement of recent times, serious and continuous attention must be paid to the movement under any of its nicknames: "radical theology," "Christian atheism," "the death of God," or "God is dead." If this attention is not given, then its potential and permanent usefulness—bringing God out of hidden corners into the full light of discussion—will be lost.

In modern Protestant theology, the figure everyone has to

confront is of course Karl Barth. I have read some of Barth (though not the whole twelve volumes of *Church Dogmatics*), and it is clear that the key to all his thought is the centrality of Jesus Christ. I have now discovered that this is an extreme position from the point of view of the whole history of Christian thought. No allowance is made by Barth, as most previous theologies have done, for knowledge that comes through nature, science, art or other sources—even if it should be guided first by the revelation in Jesus Christ.

A second significant figure behind the larger new movement in Protestant theology is Dietrich Bonhoeffer. Cultured son of a German psychiatrist, Bonhoeffer turned down asylum in the United States and returned to Germany during the Hitler regime to teach in an underground theological seminary, to write several books, and in the last days of World War II, to be killed by the Nazis.

I read Bonhoeffer's *Letters from Prison*, and they are very moving. Even more of his subsequent influence, however, derives from his unfinished *Ethics*. If we, he contended, do not pray to God for relief of pain and suffering as we formerly did, then it must follow that we do not need God in the same kind of immediate and pragmatic sense as previous ages have assumed. As far as pain and suffering are concerned we are left in a secular age and if we need relief we depend on medical science to get it. However, when we consider the entire meaning of human life itself, then we must look to God and the Christian revelation in Jesus Christ.

Bonhoeffer believed that we should stop being "religious" in the sense of believing that some special kind of activity, called "religion," such as going to church, could infallibly lead us to God, while involvement in the ordinary things of life and reflection on them could not. His criticisms of "religion," however, are no more a denial of God's reality than his statements about relief of pain and suffering are a rejection of God's concern for them.

A third great modern theologian, certainly more radical than Barth and perhaps even than Bonhoeffer, was Paul Tillich. In many of his writings, including *The Courage to Be*, Tillich declared that there can be no belief in a real God except through renouncing many other possible gods. Although I never expect to master the subtleties of Tillich's thought, I do agree with him that a smug believer in God, who never takes doubts and atheistic claims seriously, probably believes in a God who does not exist. I believe that Tillich meant, just as I found in my own life, that real belief involves a process of inquiry and not a permanently fixed position.

When Tillich, however, talks about a "God above God," about God as "ultimate concern" and as "the ground of all being," he seems to be departing from the Christian conception of a personal God.

A fourth theologian to be taken seriously is Rudolf Bultmann, who is a pioneer in demythologizing the Bible and many Christian beliefs. Among other things he is probably the principal father of John A. T. Robinson's rejection of a three-storied universe, in *Honest to God*.

A fifth important theologian of modern times is Jürgen Moltmann. In very recent years, spearheaded by him, the Theology of Hope has emerged. It is receiving respectful attention in both Europe and America. As I understand it, this movement takes the future and God's benevolent action in the future very seriously. No matter how ominous the present appears, it holds, one ought not to despair. Thus this movement calls for genuine hope in the face of much uncertainty about the future. But it relies on hope, not on the certainty of expectation. It is more realistic and attentive politically than the other recent dominant European theologies like that of Barth.

What bothers me about this movement is, first, whether it uses its vision of the future sufficiently to energize appropriate action in the present and, second, its primary emphasis on hope rather than faith.

As I read Bonhoeffer, Tillich, Bultmann, and Moltmann, and other leading theologians of our day, I could understand that each of them, in his own way, was trying to keep the Christian religion from being merely provincial or timebound or a kind of button-pressing device for man when he needs help. At the same time, I had an uncomfortable feeling that through their very sophistication they might unconsciously be moving their readers away from firm belief in a personal God—something the radical theologians are doing quite consciously.

In contrast to this trend, I sensed a trend in the other direction among some distinguished scientists, psychiatrists, and other thoughtful persons of our time. I have been especially impressed by the views on religion and God of Wernher von Braun, who finds it as difficult to understand a scientist who does not acknowledge the presence of a superior rationality behind the existence of the universe as he does to comprehend a theologian who would deny the advances of science. As reported by UPI, he finds no conflict between science and religion but sees them as "sisters." He has said, "Many people seem to feel that science has somehow made 'religious ideas' untimely or old-fashioned. But I think science has a real surprise for the skeptics."

What science has revealed about nature, says von Braun, is that "nothing can disappear without a trace. Nature does not know extinction. All it knows is transformation." He adds, "If God applies this fundamental principle to the most minute and insignificant parts of his universe, doesn't it make sense to assume that he applies it also to the human soul? I think it does."

Another great scientist, James A. Van Allen, discoverer of the Van Allen radiation belt, said in his commencement address at Butler University on June 12, 1966: "Science is completely impoverished in those aspects of life which transcend the limits of strict rationality—love and trust and fidelity and hope—those very aspects which illuminate and give meaning and fullness to life. If I were required to choose between science and divinity, my decision would be instantaneous, and science would be a clearly second choice."

Having studied the standard and radical theologians, I inquired as to whether there has been any other kind of attempt to reconsider the question of God's reality and nature in recent years. The most intriguing quests appear in the work of Alfred North Whitehead, Charles Hartshorne, Schubert M. Ogden, and some related figures.

As I understand it, they are all "process" theologians, which means that they regard yesterday's substantive categories as likely to mislead us today. In some appropriate way, then, they see God as involved with the specific processes of our world and our lives in a much more thoroughgoing fashion than older theologies assumed. What this group seems mainly concerned with is the manner in which God works. Process theology does not throw out God; but the models by which we understand God and his work, it contends, must be brought up to date.

These theologians impress me with their contention that creative new ways of thinking about God, in keeping with the process views of the universe that science has made necessary, are possible without destroying the spiritual and psychological values of our older notions of God in His creative and redemptive activity. We can, they tell us, rethink God without declaring Him dead!

These thoughts about God, about atheisms new and old, and about the present Protestant rethinking of God, are rudimentary. I have made no reference to the ontological, the cosmological, or the teleological arguments in favor of God's existence, nor to any of the systems dealing with what He is like. I am dissatisfied with all the formal proofs, and I have nothing new and convincing—except experience resulting in belief—to put in their place. I do believe in a God who is eternal, who creates us daily as well as having done so from the beginning, and who has given revelations to us which we neglect at our own loss.

I also believe that God has given us real though limited freedom, that he respects our critical thinking and does not damn us for doubting and inquiring, and that He is, finally, less concerned about our acknowledging Him than He is with how we deal with our fellow man and with ourselves. I find the worship of God of great importance to me. But this is not because God is "narcissistic." He could get along without praise from me. But my life, of myself and in my relationships, needs contact with Him, especially in the discipline, confession, and adoration of worship.

I remember, however, that approach to the God who is really God must involve a constant renunciation of the gods who threaten the true God. Therefore, even the "God Is Dead" movement may help to expose the false gods. There are many caricatures of God constructed by limited human vision that I too want to bury. But I believe there is a real God who is not dead.

Princeton Theological Seminary had done a splendid job with the World Religions Conferences, and when I reflected on my concern about the Death of God movement in Christian theology and about the meaning of new forms of atheism, it occurred to me that perhaps Princeton might also be interested in sponsoring a conference, supported by me, that would attempt a high-level evaluation of thinking about God, including the extreme views of the radical theologians. Princeton accepted this proposal, and excellent planning for the conference was done by Hugh Thomson Kerr, professor of theology and editor of *Theology Today* magazine.

The conference convened for four days in Princeton during April of 1968. I was much disappointed that I could not attend personally, but at that time I was having a siege of arthritis in my back; however, I received copies of the papers that were presented, along with tape recordings of the proceedings which included the criticism of each paper and ensuing discussion. Further, Seward Hiltner visited me after the conference and, also, I talked at some length with my minister, who had been present at Princeton.

I was again intrigued to see what occurs when outstanding theological scholars meet for a discussion. First, I was deeply impressed with their scholarly knowledge and insight; secondly, with how much their opinions differed. Here was the elite of Christian theological scholars, each with a great reputation and a following of his own, and yet, there was no consensus as to the future course of Christian theology or the Christian Church; lastly, I saw once more how much easier it is to be a critic of any system, dogma, doctrine, or belief than it is to offer something more constructive.

The theme of the sessions was "Next Steps for Church and Theology." The morning and afternoon sessions were limited to the conference membership, while evening sessions were open to the public. The latter included addresses by Bishop John A.

T. Robinson of London and Professor Jürgen Moltmann of Tubingen, Germany.

The conference membership consisted of about fifty people. It included almost all the radical theologians, several Roman Catholic theologians including two representatives of the Vatican, and most of the well-known Protestant theologians in the United States. A number of people have since told me with appreciation that so diverse a group had never before been brought together for a dialogue in depth.

The central tension point of the discussions focused on the kind of relationship that should exist between tradition on the one hand and flexibility on the other. No one was completely on one side or the other, and there were wide variations in emphasis. Even among the Catholic theologians, there seemed general agreement that theology can no longer simply use the old forms, structures, and categories. And, conversely, radical theologians showed a serious respect for tradition.

I was impressed by John A. T. Robinson's two definitions of "radical." The correct one, he believes, by analogy with the roots of a tree, seeks to relate to its far-flung and deep roots and not to deny them. The second and improper meaning would be to uproot the tradition altogether. Most of the conference members seemed to side with Bishop Robinson on this point.

What struck me most forcibly was the emphasis on the need to construct a new "theological anthropology," that is, a new emphasis on man in the light of God and the Christian tradition, and fully open to the contributions the sciences have made and will make to our understanding of man's individual and social fulfillment. This seemed of special significance in view of the fact that, in Karl Barth's theological system, there is no special category reserved for "anthropology." In suggesting that the next real step in theology focus on anthropology, Albert C. Outler made it clear that he wanted neither a "baptizing" of scientific findings without reference to the uniqueness of Christianity nor a theology superimposed upon man without taking the sciences seriously.

At this point I realized that I was witnessing some kind of merger between my earlier interest in the relation of religion to psychiatry and my more recent interest in theology. For psychiatric findings are certainly among the most important for a theological anthropology to consult. The older theologies that saw Freud, for instance, only as a threat, are well buried. Freud ought not to be "baptized," but his findings and his views are illuminative of man's nature.

In the discussion of the church, the lines were drawn between those favoring "renewal" (real and even radical change but not breaking continuity with the tradition and the institution) and the smaller number apparently in favor of discarding all traditional forms such as the local church. No one was merely in favor of the ecclesiastical status quo. Yet Peter Berger, speaking against the more revolutionary thoughts, expressed the opinion that, with confusion now rife in our society, it is important for the church to stand as a conserving and stabilizing force.

There was a similar division of conviction in the discussion of Christian ethics. Should Christians align themselves with revolutionary social forces all across the world and help to overthrow unjust structures of society, by force if need be? Or should they try to produce change without violent revolutions?

One of the conference surprises was the views of the Roman Catholic theologians, both priests and laymen. I knew, of course, that there was a new openness to inquiry and change in the Catholic Church. What I had not realized before, however, was that there are some "radical theologians" in that church—radical in Bishop Robinson's sense of going back to the roots and criticizing everything from that perspective. To be sure, the long traditions of both Catholicism and Protestantism are sufficiently different that it will be years before common ground rules for discussion of many issues can be set up. But at the conference, it was astonishing how similarly the Protestants and Catholics saw the current issues.

Conferences involve, after all, not just issues and discussion but people. In the discussions, I was greatly impressed with Albert C. Outler. Scholarly as he is, he was nevertheless the first critic of the tendency of theological discussion to become an esoteric exercise in which specialists talk only to each other.

The ability of Harvey Cox, both in his paper and in the

discussions, was clearly evident. His trenchant analysis in *The Secular City* makes more sense to me after this conference. At one point in the discussion Cox admitted that he was more "orthodox" than some thought.

Thomas J. J. Altizer impressed me more positively in this conference than through his works. While he is still some kind of Death-of-God theologian, he clearly was not conducting funeral services at Princeton. I was more impressed than ever with the personal and theological integrity of William Hamilton. With Outler, he saw the next theological step as "anthropology," and I thought him wise in suggesting that we are just now at the "milling around" stage.

John A. T. Robinson's *Honest to God* had struck me positively in his attempt to help us think about God as modern men and not as ancients, but I had wondered if he were not actually getting rid of God, even though at the conference he stated that he is radical only in the sense of his own previously cited definition, of retracing our roots and criticizing in the light of those roots.

Peter Berger displayed one of the sharpest and most practical minds of the entire conference. On one occasion he asked if we were not endangered today by having "mood theologies," which react so much to the immediate situation that they fail to bring the wisdom of history to bear upon current problems.

Schubert M. Ogden impressed me as one of the ablest younger theologians with his process emphasis in theology. His kind of thinking, along with that of John Cobb in "natural theology," will undoubtedly provide one of the bridges between traditional theologies and the more extreme ones of today.

In retrospect I am gratified that the course of my own theological pilgrimage led me to propose this conference, and that James I. McCord and Hugh Thomson Kerr were able to assemble this unprecedented group of theological brains.

Where, now, do I stand theologically? In terms of actual convictions, not very far from where I stood before. I discovered that many of my own early and current questionings, however naïve in form, are of serious interest to the best theological minds of our day. To be sure, the scholars' knowledge is encyclopedic and their terminology more scholarly and sophisticated, but they are wrestling with the same basic questions as I. I realize too that, in theology just as in science, major advances are made through periods of confusion and uncertainty, as happened in science, for instance, under the impact of Einstein's theories.

As for the future of the Christian Church, some things appear to me to be elementary. Important though church headquarters are in New York, Geneva, Rome, and elsewhere, the future of the church will depend on how it operates at the local level. The Bible must be skillfully interpreted and the worship services made relevant to today's world. Starting at an early age in Sunday school, we should phase out teaching fundamentalism. We cannot teach our children the scientific proof of evolution five days a week and teach the Adam and Eve myth as a historical fact on Sunday. The contents of books like Fosdick's *Modern Use of the Bible* and *Guide to Understanding the Bible* should be a part of religious education on all levels. Otherwise a great number of our youth will continue to be disillusioned with the Christian religion and alienated from the church at one of the most crucial periods of their lives. When they react against some of the incredible Bible stories and much outdated Christian theology, they start looking elsewhere for the purpose and meaning of life. Quite often this causes our college students to try and find their answers through pure reason. If they pursue this path far enough in depth, they wind up even more frustrated and disillusioned, because science has no answers about life's meaning or purpose.

By this time a majority of students have become disillusioned on both fronts—Christianity on the one hand and science on the other, and they either become cynics or stoics and give up the search altogether; or they make a game of digging up every idea and thought about meaning and purpose from all the world cultures since the dawn of civilization. If this appears to be an overstatement, I would like to quote from an article by Huston Smith, professor of philosophy at MIT, about his experience with eight MIT upper classmen that formed a preceptoral group:

It was to be an independent study project which the students were to conduct themselves; my role was to be that of adviser and consultant. Ostensibly on Asian thought, it began respectably enough with standard texts from the Chinese and Indian traditions, but, as the weeks moved on and the students' true interests surfaced, the original syllabus began to lurch and reel. . . . I cannot recall the exact progression of topics, but it went something like this: Beginning with Asian philosophy, it moved on to meditation, then yoga, then Zen, then Tibet, then successively to the *Bardo Thodol*, tantra, the kundalini, the chakras, the *I Ching*, karati and aikido, the yang-yin macrobiotic (brown rice) diet, Gurdjieff, Maher Baba, astrology, astral bodies, auras, UFO's, Tarot cards, parapsychology, witchcraft, and magic. And underlying everything, of course, the psychedelic drugs.[30]

Dr. Paul W. Pruyser, eminent psychologist, has this to say about Smith's article, "There is good and bad mysticism, primitive and sophisticated myth, clever and poor poetry, etc. Why settle for poor myth, flimsy mysticism, lousy poetry if better alternatives are available? . . . Moreover, there are abundant signs that these clever minds (with high IQs and excellent science training) have been left half-barbarian in regard to humanistic ideals, sense of history, discernment in matters of art, literature and poetry, discipline that used to stem from contact with classical languages and authors."[31]

Here I think we find the dilemma of millions of our young people. They can't find the answers they seek in orthodox Christian theology, and they can't find them in science, so they bounce off in every conceivable direction and reexamine everything from antiquity to the present, in some cases with minds distorted through the use of drugs. However, I am sure they won't find their answers by a flight into mysticism, particularly when it takes such a regressive form. Many of their studies are so bizarre and abstruse that they are difficult to understand, yet stupid to believe, a paradox of intellectual acuity and nonsense.

Shortly after reading Huston Smith's article and Paul Pruyser's comments, I had the pleasure of spending an evening with Dr. Smith at my home after he had given the commencement address for Gloria's graduating class at Tudor Hall School. I was glad that Gloria had a chance to hear him at her formative age of seventeen because he is not only a great scholar but seems to have great insight into the minds and emotions of young people.

Youth is just one problem the church is faced with, but probably the most crucial since one half of our population is twenty-six or under, and in just twenty-one years children yet unborn will be of age and at our rate of growth, will be a majority in the United States. The Christian Church is not solely responsible for what the next generation will become, but it certainly has a primary responsibility and a golden opportunity. Yet we are running out of time. Christians are a minority in the world, and they soon will be in America if the trend isn't reversed. Many knowledgeable scholars are already talking of the post-Christian era.

We are faced with a crisis in belief in this country that is fast approaching a relative code of ethics that "nothing is good or bad but thinking makes it so,"[32] and, when we reach this point, we aren't far from dismissing God entirely; and then, as Dostoyevsky said in *The Brothers Karamazov*, "all is permitted." Such an outlook can lead only to anarchy, and anarchy is inevitably followed by some form of tyranny.

While I think that a crisis in belief is our primary problem, doing good works in the world is not far behind. In a broader sense, the greatest problem of the church is to find a proper balance between the two. The local church is a university of life; and while it can emphasize some aspects, depending on its environment, it cannot focus exclusively on any one phase without losing its identity. It is easy for a church to fall into the trap of focusing exclusively on a single problem such as civil rights, poverty, pastoral counseling, juvenile delinquency, old age, etc., or to turn its back on all these human problems and focus exclusively on worship.

God is both transcendent and immanent. To fulfill its destiny, the church must move in *both* directions, maintaining a strong emphasis on worship while it carries on good works inside and outside the church. It is not a case of either/or, as each complements and strengthens the other. The church can furnish a sanctuary for reflection and inspiration and fortify faith in lasting values; and, in turn, the members working on human needs can carry out what the church stands for.

We must also remember that, while all the local churches are subject to the above criteria, the specifics of their worship service and good works will vary depending on their location and the makeup of their congregations. The famous Riverside Church in New York City, with its mixed congregation and close proximity to Harlem, would face problems quite different from those of a church in the small town of Syracuse, Indiana. The Riverside Church is surrounded by racial problems and poverty, yet the church in Syracuse has no racial problem in the entire community and no abject poverty. However, the members of both churches worship the same God and share in the same existential problems of life—divorce, juvenile delinquency, alcoholism, mental illness, old age, pain, suffering, and death. Thus all churches, wherever located, in the inner city, suburbia, or in rural communities, have a mission that is universal.

"It has been said that most of the churches in the land are well filled but, we are told, they are filled for the wrong reasons. Those who write books about the church today explain that people fill pews and rosters out of fear or self-righteousness, to enhance reputation in the community or to restore a sagging self-esteem, to develop professional and business contacts or to escape from the tribulations of profession and business. We are told that people go in search of guaranteed friendships or psychological refurbishing at less cost than country club or psychiatrist, or just because—like raising three children in a split-level house with a weedless front yard—it's 'the thing to do.' "[33] The suburban churches have been particularly criticized for insulating themselves from human problems.

While it is no doubt true that some of the criticism is justified, the much maligned suburban churches have great potential, and many are already fulfilling their responsibilities. Although the suburban church itself is not located in the inner city physically, its members largely represent the power structure in the inner city, and the parish minister is in a strategic position to humanize all aspects of the secular city by inspiring his members. In fact, many suburban churches are serving this purpose now, unheralded and unsung.

It would be impossible for the church as a body to take over major good works in a secular world. It doesn't have the money or the professional experts needed in every area of human need; and, even then, it would be duplicating what is now done by other organizations and governmental units. However, the church can and must serve as a focal point and nerve center to reach into every human need and every layer of industry, labor, race, and poverty through its membership. If it were possible to dramatize church membership in the secular world on a control panel, the skeptics would be amazed at the thousands of lights that would go on daily throughout any city. Choose any good cause in any community, and you will usually find that most of the leadership and volunteer workers on all levels are church members.

In summary, I believe the Christian Church, with all its fallibilities and shortcomings, offers the best hope for man. Self-criticism is constructive, but the church has gone overboard with apologies and confessions of guilt and sin on some human problems, almost to the point of mass masochism or psychological sickness. Yet the church has always been the center of worship and has an endless record of good works. In the field of health and education alone, it has organized most of the private hospitals, colleges, and universities. On the whole, it has a right to be proud of its heritage, and I am convinced it has a destiny of indispensable service to fulfill.

As I reflected on the conferences at the Menninger Foundation and Princeton, I began to realize how much insight I had gained, both directly and indirectly; directly, as a result of the papers delivered, the ensuing discussions and personal conversations with great scholars, and indirectly, by the reading they stimulated me to do and the flow of ideas that followed. My life has often been confused and some of it tragic, but suddenly I realized the deep wisdom of Aristotle, that meaning is better revealed in the end than it is in the beginning. I saw that after all the commercial and personal struggles, all the painful search for purpose and meaning, these made sense only if, conjointly, they contributed to a purpose larger than my own life.

NOTES

Chapter 2

1. Shakespeare, *Julius Caesar*, IV, 3
   (London: The Macmillan Co., Ltd., 1930), p. 340
2. Shakespeare, *Hamlet*, IV, 5
   (London: The Macmillan Co., Ltd., 1930), p. 535

Chapter 3

3. Shakespeare, *Macbeth*, IV, 1
   (London: The Macmillan Co., Ltd., 1930), p. 365
4. Hendrik Van Loon, *The Story of the Bible*
   (New York: Garden City Publishing Co., Inc., 1941), p. 277
5. Kahlil Gibran, *The Prophet*
   (New York: Alfred A. Knopf, 1957), p. 33

Chapter 4

6. Shakespeare, *Hamlet*, II, 2
   (London: The Macmillan Co., Ltd., 1930), p. 452

Chapter 5

7. Anderson House—National Headquarters and Museum of the Society of the Cincinnati, Washington, D.C.

Chapter 6

8. H. E. Fosdick, *The Modern Use of the Bible*
   (New York: The Macmillan Co., 1945), p. 4
9. H. E. Fosdick, *A Guide to Understanding the Bible*
   (New York and London: Harper & Brothers, 1938), p. 53
10. Whitney J. Oates, *Basic Writings of Saint Augustine*
    (New York & Toronto, Canada: Random House, 1948), p. xvi Intro.
11. William James, *Essays on Faith and Morals*
    (New York, London, Toronto: Longman's, Green & Co., 1947), p. 44
12. Robert Bretall, *A Kierkegaard Anthology*
    (Princeton, N.J.: Princeton University Press, 1951), p. xxv Intro.
13. *Ibid*, p. xxi
14. William James, *The Varieties of Religious Experience*
    (London, New York, Toronto: Longman's, Green & Co., 1928), p. 73
15. H. E. Fosdick, *The Living of These Days*
    (New York: Harper & Brothers, 1956), p. 269
16. *Reader's Digest*, February, 1950
    (Pleasantville, N.Y. & Canada, 1950), pp. 116, 117

Chapter 7

17. Voltaire, *The Best of All Possible Worlds*
    (New York: The Vanguard Press, 1929), p. 223
18. The original on which the anonymous parody is based is by James Ball Naylor and appears in:
    John Bartlett, *Familiar Quotations*
    (Boston: Little, Brown & Co., 11th Edition, 1939), pp. 754, 755

Chapter 8

19. Smiley Blanton with Arthur Gordon, *Now or Never*
    (Englewood Cliffs, N.J.: Prentice-Hall, Inc., 1959), p. 8
20. Shakespeare, *As You Like It*, II, 7
    (London: The Macmillan Co., Ltd., 1930), p. 498

Chapter 9

21. David Neiswanger, *Presidential address*
    (Menninger Foundation Annual Meeting, 1955)
22. Heinz Haber, *Our Friend the Atom*
    (New York: Golden Press, 1961), p. 112
23. *Ibid*, p. 116
24. *Ibid*, p. 128
25. *Ibid*, pp. 146–47
26. Lincoln Barnett, *The Universe and Dr. Einstein*
    (New York: William Sloane Associates, 1957), p. 33
27. *Ibid*, p. 69
28. *Ibid*, p. 69
29. *Ibid*, p. 1

Chapter 10

30. Huston Smith, "Secularization and the Sacred: The Contemporary Scene,"
    The Religious Situation: 1968, ed. Donald Cutler (Boston: Beacon Press,
    1968), p. 594.
31. Undated personal letter to E. F. Gallahue
32. Shakespeare, *Hamlet*, II, 2
    (London: The Macmillan Co., Ltd., 1930), p. 452
33. James E. Dittes, *The Church in the Way*
    (New York: Charles Scribner's Sons, 1967), p. v Preface

BIBLIOGRAPHY

Thomas J. J. Altizer, *The Gospel of Christian Atheism* (Philadelphia: The Westminster Press, 1966).

Thomas J. J. Altizer and William Hamilton, *Radical Theology and the Death of God* (Indianapolis: Bobbs-Merrill Publishing Co., 1966).

Karl Barth, *Church Dogmatics* (Edinburgh: T. & T. Clark, 1936–1962, 12 vols.).

Arthur Beckhard, *Albert Einstein* (New York: G. P. Putnam's Sons, 1959).

Dietrich Bonhoeffer, *Ethics* (New York: The Macmillan Co., 1955).

———, *Letters and Papers from Prison* (London: SCM Press, 1953).

John B. Cobb, *A Christian Natural Theology* (Philadelphia: The Westminster Press, 1965).

James A. Coleman, *Relativity for the Layman* (New York: William Frederick Press, 1958).

Will Durant, *The Story of Philosophy* (New York: Simon and Schuster, 1933).

Sigmund Freud, *The Future of an Illusion* (New York: Anchor Books, 1964).

Charles Hartshorne, *The Divine Relativity, a Social Conception* (New Haven: Yale University Press, 1948).

Seward Hiltner and Karl Menninger, Eds., *Constructive Aspects of Anxiety* (New York: Abingdon Press, 1963).

William Ernest Hocking, *Living Religions and a World Faith* (London: Allen and Unwin, 1940).

Robert E. Hume, *The World's Living Religions* (New York: Charles Scribner's Sons, 1924).

Carl G. Jung, *Modern Man in Search of a Soul* (New York: Harcourt, Brace & World, 1955).

Edward J. Jurji, Ed., *The Great Religions of the Modern World* (Princeton: University Press, 1946).

Sören Kierkegaard, *Edifying Discourses* (New York: Harper & Row, 1958).

Hendrik Kramer, *World Cultures and World Religions: The Coming Dialogue* (London: Lutterworth Press, 1960).

Gabriel Marcel, *Homo Viator* (New York: Harper and Row, 1965).

Karl Menninger, *The Vital Balance* (New York: The Viking Press, 1963).

William C. Menninger, *Psychiatry: Its Evolution and Present Status* (Ithaca: Cornell University Press, 1948).

Jürgen Moltmann, *Theology of Hope* (New York: Harper & Row, 1967).

Friedrich Nietzsche, *Thus Spake Zarathustra* (New York: The Macmillan Co., 1906).

———, *The Will to Power* (New York: Random House, 1967).

Schubert M. Ogden, *Christ Without Myth* (New York: Harper and Row, 1961).

———, *The Reality of God and Other Essays* (New York: Harper and Row, 1966).

Constance M. Pott, *Francis Bacon and his Secret Society*, 1891 (New York: AMS Publishers).

John A. T. Robinson, *Honest to God* (Philadelphia: The Westminster Press, 1963).

Leroy S. Rouner, *Philosophy, Religion, and the Coming World Civilization: Essays in Honor of W. E. Hocking* (The Hague: M. Nijhoff, 1966).

Jean Paul Sartre, *Existentialism* (New York: Philosophical Library, 1947).

Arthur Schopenhauer, *Essays of Schopenhauer* (New York: Willey Book Company).

———, *On the Basis of Morality* (Indianapolis: Bobbs-Merrill Co., 1965).

Paul Tillich, *The Courage to Be* (New Haven: Yale University Press, 1952).

Arnold Toynbee, *Christianity Among the Religions of the World* (New York: Charles Scribner's Sons, 1957).

D. Elton Trueblood, *The Logic of Belief* (New York: Harper and Row, 1942).

Paul Van Buren, *The Secular Meaning of the Gospel* (New York: The Macmillan Co., 1963).

Alfred North Whitehead, *Process and Reality* (New York: The Macmillan Co., 1929).

L